Folklife

ANNUAL 88-89

A Publication of the

AMERICAN FOLKLIFE CENTER

AT THE LIBRARY OF CONGRESS

Edited by James Hardin and Alan Jabbour

LIBRARY OF CONGRESS· WASHINGTON· 1989

Folklife Annual presents a yearly collection of articles
on American traditional expressive life. Articles on
folklife in other countries are included when they have
implications for the study of folklife in this country.
The articles are written by specialists in folklife and
related fields, but the annual is intended for a wide
audience. A publication of the American Folklife Cen-
ter at the Library of Congress, Folklife Annual seeks
to promote the documentation and study of American
folklife, share the traditions, values, and activities of
American folk culture with many people, and serve as
a national forum for the discussion of ideas and issues
in folklore and folklife.

Articles may be submitted for consideration to
the Editors, Folklife Annual, American Folklife Cen-
ter, the Library of Congress, Washington, D.C. 20540.
Manuscripts should be typewritten, double-spaced,
and in accord with the Chicago Manual of Style.

Cover: Mary Vanderhorst
sews a sweetgrass basket in
the small shed behind her
roadside stand on Highway
17, Mt. Pleasant, South
Carolina. Photograph by
David A. Taylor, March
1987

Title page: Baskets by
Florence Mazyck and her
daughters, at a basket
stand along Highway 17,
near Mt. Pleasant, South
Carolina. Photograph by
Darcy Wingfield, 1985.
Courtesy of the McKissick
Museum

For sale by the Superintendent of Documents,
U.S. Government Printing Office,
Washington, D.C. 20402
ISBN 0-8444-0638-4
ISSN 0747-5322

Designed by Adrianne Onderdonk Dudden

*"The Threshing Floor."
Watercolor by Alice Rave-
nel Huger Smith. Courtesy
of the Carolina Art Asso-
ciation/Gibbes Museum of
Art, Charleston, South
Carolina*

Folklife Annual 1988–89 is dedicated to the
American Folklore Society in its centennial year.
The society was founded in Cambridge, Massachusetts,
in 1888 and held its first annual meeting
in Philadelphia, Pennsylvania, in 1889.

Contents

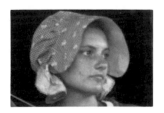

Preface

America is a nation of immigrants, of people willing (or in some cases forced) to leave old lives and start new ones, attracted by the promises of an imagined land. We are also a nation of movers, historically ready to "light out for the territory," as Huck Finn did when he sensed Aunt Sally's imminent attempts to "sivilize" him. As the country developed and "manifest destiny" became a national slogan, our restless journeys continued, and we found ourselves traveling a tripartite landscape divided into regions of civilization, frontier, and wilderness.

Cities, towns, and farming communities have provided social and cultural opportunities for many. But for others, the Huckleberry Finns among us, those civilized regions confine and deaden the spirit. The original American wilderness, that great stretch of forest, mountain, prairie, and plain, has both frightened and fired imaginations with its sense of freedom and lack of boundaries. Europe's folklore, and later our own, peopled it with demons on the one hand and noble savages on the other. The wilderness was actually a place of both beauty and danger—the experience of it more and less than imagined expectations—and the mountain men who survived its rigors were themselves full of wildness and often less than admirable characters.

The pioneer settlers we celebrate in poetry and song were headed not for wilderness but for the frontier. In Europe the frontier is the boundary between two civilized nations. In America, the frontier was a transitional zone (between civilization and wilderness; between culture and nature), a vague, unfinished region where land was cheap and abundant, attitudes and ways of doing things loose, and resourcefulness a primary value. By 1890, the U.S. Census reported, the country was so broken up by settlement that a frontier zone no longer existed.

But the frontier still lingers in the American imagination, where it provides, in Daniel Boorstin's figure, a "fertile verge" to all the endeavors of American culture. And the battle between Huck and Aunt Sally continues within us and bursts forth across those remaining regions of land, sea, or sky beyond civilization.

Some of these imagined projections are registered in the articles in this year's *Folklife Annual:* Mary Hufford shows that the voices of hounds on a foxchase generate a unique set of landscapes in the minds of the listening hunters. Jane Schwartz records the way city residents engaged in pigeon flying temporarily escape the confines of brick and asphalt as they release their flocks into the boundless space above the rooftops. David Whisnant puzzles over the misconception by outsiders of one landscape in the past; and Erika Brady describes the collision between competing conceptions in another landscape today.

In her article, Brady says that visitors to an Ozark national forest sometimes enact a return to an imagined wilderness (safe from the dangers of an earlier one), offending residents and thus raising the issue that informs many of the articles in this year's annual—the relations between local people and outsiders visiting a region. During the time of European settlement, American land was advertised, sometimes in exaggerated fashion, to attract settlers; later, areas were promoted as sites for both development and tourism. Marta Weigle discusses the state promotional guidebooks written during the thirties under the auspices of the Federal Writers' Project, and shows that the guide for New Mexico stressed local folk culture as a way to attract tourists. Today, the National Park Service must wrestle with the problem of how to manage a region so that it can be enjoyed without being destroyed, a kind of golden-goose dilemma.

The development and tourism around Charleston, South Carolina, has been a mixed blessing for the makers of sea grass baskets. Dale Rosengarten outlines the irony that an influx of people provided a new market for the baskets, but that development sometimes destroys the sea grass used to make them. Terry Zug describes a North Carolina potter who adapted his craft to the requests of outsiders and was thus able to stay in business. Aesthetic considerations succeeded where utilitarian ones failed for potter Burlon Craig and enabled him to keep a traditional craft alive. In Philadelphia, utility is still the chief objective of a Hmong basketmaker, but he has not gained the recognition accorded some folk artists because of the non-traditional material he employs, plastic straps.

As "civilization" gains ground in our tripartite American landscape, a number of questions confront us: Should the traditional ways of earlier times be kept alive or allowed to die, as they outlive their usefulness? What aspects of the cultures of our newest immigrants should be or can be imported and maintained here? Is it possible for traditional customs to thrive in changing contexts? Do they become something different in translation? How are artifacts like Burlon Craig's pots to be regarded when they are made primarily for collectors? These are the teasing questions raised by the articles that follow. And somehow the descriptions of fraktur and reverse glass painting offered by Don Yoder and Ervin Beck seem homey and comfortable in their midst. These artistic expressions are produced for, by, and within communities whose people accept them as their own. But Pamela Swing shows that even in a conservative and traditional community, extraordinary means may be necessary to ensure the continuance of a traditional folk art. In the Shetland Isles, it took a gifted teacher and the non-traditional methods of the classroom to revitalize traditional fiddle playing.

For whatever reasons of utility or beauty a tourist or collector is inspired to travel to a natural or culturally exotic landscape or to purchase a folk cultural artifact, one element of attraction is in the power to evoke an earlier time of challenge and individual resourcefulness. As we dream and create, we continue to seek out or gather in images of our historic ability to respond to and subdue the American landscape.

JH

The editors would like to thank David A. Taylor for his help with this year's annual.

Casting the hounds ahead of the pickup. "We road hunt 'em," said Norman Taylor, "until they find a fox." Photograph by Mary Hufford, November 1980

Soundscape and Story

Foxhunting in New Jersey's Pine Barrens

BY MARY HUFFORD

While foxhunters in New Jersey's Lebanon State Forest warm their hands on a chill December morning, the woods around them ring with canine "descriptions" of the fox's course through the Pine Barrens landscape. Photograph by Mary Hufford, 1980

> *"It's kind of funny. Foxhunters don't really hunt fox. They don't shoot them. They run dogs. That's the real fun for them."*
> —Christian Bethmann,
> *Lebanon State Forest Superintendent,*
> *September 21, 1983*

Day is breaking on Lebanon State Forest, breaking on the Mount Misery Brook and its tributaries, and on the swamps, streams, "spongs," and bogs that slope gently away from them into pine-studded uplands laced with sand roads. It breaks on the blue jays and towhees whose cries punctuate the deep January silence, and it breaks on the cold, meandering trails of foxes bedding down for the day.

The Pine Barrens is in its winter aspect. White sand roads, carpeted with amber pine needles, travel past the red spikes of sweet huck, the grays of soap bushes, and yellow-brown hues of scrub oak. Behind and around these the evergreen sheep laurel, cedar, and pine rise and taper off into a fathomless blue sky. Against such a backdrop the movements of "parti-colored" foxhounds, black and brown and splashed with white, leap quickly to the hunter's eye.

Along the branches of the Mount Misery Brook the silence is about to end. On the North Branch Road a pickup truck crawls slowly along surrounded by hounds busily inspecting the roadside flora. Over on Reeves's Bog Road another hunter has just turned off the headlights on a pickup full of foxhounds. And on the Blacktop Road a truck door slams, a tailgate squeaks open, and a handful of hounds bursts into the road. At this point in a chase, hunters say, the ears of foxes prick up.

On the roof of each pickup cab is a CB antenna. The first hunter to strike a fox's line will notify the others. Meanwhile they coordinate their reconnaissance, using CB aliases.

Yellow Bird contacts Dogman.

"Hey Dogman, how 'boutcha Dogman, Dogman?"

"I gotcha."

"What's your 10-4?"[1]

"I got tracks goin' out toward North Branch Road right now. I'm on North Branch Road."

"Where'd Horsetrader go?"

"Reeves's Bogs Road."

"Okay, I'll go right up South Branch towards the head of it then."

"All right."

On the back of each pickup is a large "dog box," its wooden sides attached to the truck walls. Each box contains a dozen or more hounds, their nails scrabbling on the hard metal floor of the truck bed, some of them peering out through the bars over the tailgate. These are Maryland fox hounds, born and bred to chase foxes on the Atlantic Coastal Plain. Their noses are constantly sniffing, evaluating and dismissing, casting about for the scent of fox. One hound, yearning to join the nascent chase at South Branch Bogs, begins to whine anxiously, a high nasal whine reminiscent of brakes needing adjustment.

"Shush! Maggie!" Norman Taylor admonishes her. He is a ruddy, pleasant-faced man, sturdily built, in his mid-sixties, whose red hair is turning to white. His surname has been in the region since the early nineteenth century, when his grandfather, Capt. Miles Standish Taylor, quit a seafaring career to settle along the coast. Reeves

Yellow Bird uses his CB radio to confer with Dog Man, as they coordinate their hounds' ranging search for a fox trail, called a cast. Photograph by Dennis McDonald, January 1989

Years ago foxhunters started calling him "Yellow Bird," after the color of his truck.

Written on the side of the pickup at Middle Branch is the name of the hunter there: Theodore Bell, Jr., Wrightstown, New Jersey. His friends call him Junie, but foxhunters call him Dogman, because he keeps a large pack of hounds, all females. His hat has a foxhound on it, under the word *Foxhunter,* and a standing fox decal is pasted to his dog box. Retirement from his job as superintendent of custodians for the Northern Burlington school system is a few years away, and he cannot get out to hunt as often as he would like, but he goes evenings and weekends, every chance he gets. Carol, his wife, sits in the cab, knitting, as she always does when accompanying him on fox chases. On weekdays she drives a school bus.

ancestors, on his mother's side, were interred in local cemeteries before the Revolutionary War. Lebanon State Forest is now a patch of wilderness, preserved by the state for recreational and scientific use. However, to Norman, who grew up in and around these woods with four brothers and eight sisters, Lebanon State Forest is more like a backyard dotted with remnants of family workscapes: swamps that Norman lumbered with his father, George "Topsy" Taylor, cranberry bogs that they labored in, and sawmills, some of them water-powered, where they made crates for cranberries and blueberries, and shingles for houses.

In 1983 Norman retired from his job of twenty-eight years as maintenance supervisor for Burlington County, reaching a state in life he had long anticipated. "That's what I worked for all these years," he once said, "To retire to foxhunt. I'm gonna enjoy it 'til I kick the bucket." (Interview, Aug. 12, 1982)[2] The hood ornament on his Toyota pickup truck is a fox in flight and a standing red fox appears over the visor on his cap.

Hounds on a cold trail emit a long drawn-out "bawl note," indicating that a fox has been through the woods, but they have not "started" or "jumped" it. A smart hound soon learns to recognize a "backfoot"—that is, the fox's trail backwards—by the weakening scent. The hounds can tell they are headed in the right direction when the scent gets stronger, and when the scent gets stronger the voices get louder.

"Can you identify all the notes?" I ask Norman.

"Oh sure, I know all of 'em. That long high note is Sailor: 'Aiooo! Aiooo!' he says. Smoke has got a nice—'Barooo!'—strong note. And Nip—'Arwoohr!'—is the big coarse note."

Rarely are hounds said to bark. Rather, they yell, squall, scream, boo-hoo, babble, holler, tongue, lie, sing, talk, and crow. A dog may be said to have a "tenor mouth," "horn chop," or "double yell," or be a "drum dog," "heavy-noted," "bass-noted," "turkey-mouthed," "parrot-mouthed," or "squealy-mouthed."

"There's a crowing note," said Milton Collins, a Methodist minister from Port Republic whose avocation is foxhunting:

Just like a rooster crowing. That's an unusual one. Then there is a high shrill whistle type. That's another thrilling thing. That's what my young dog had when he was a puppy, and when that young dog would hit a fox he'd just make your hair stand on end. But the older he got, the lower the pitch became, see? Then there's a chop: "Chop-chop-chop-chop!" And then there's a screaming note. A gyp many times will have a screaming note. And there's all in between. Mike, he's got a *heavy*, heavy chop, but you can't hear him as far as the gyp that's got the shrill. (Interview, Dec. 18, 1980)

A very few hounds possess the coveted "bugle" mouth.

Norman's Lead, a hound he had in the early fifties, had a bugle mouth. "He had the greatest voice you ever heard in your life," Norman recalled. "They made a movie called *The Voice of Bugle Ann,* and this dog had a better voice. Music flowed out of him."

"What was his voice like?" I asked him on several occasions.

"Just like a high roll," he replied:

Really high, and he could use it all the time. He wasn't the kind of dog that just used it here and there. It just filled the air, and that's all you could hear. . . . Sound just like a fire engine siren goin' off. And he could hold it long like that: "Aroooooo!" I've run him with as high as a hundred hounds, and you could always hear him. It just seemed like you could hear the roll over all. (Interview, Aug. 2, 1982)

But a mixture of voices is required for a symphonic effect, to make each hound's part in a chase discernible. Norman likened a pack of hounds to a band, with bass, tenor, and soprano voices. "By puttin' em all together," he said, "it's what makes your fox chase, and it's what makes your music good." (Interview, Jan. 22, 1986)

Beyond contributing to the aural pleasure of the hunters, the voices are also the scoreboard of the hunt, telling the hunters where the dogs are on the landscape, and their positions relative to each other and to the fox, whose objectives include making them "check" or "miss." "You can tell just how close they're runnin' to the fox by their

Official visitor's map of Lebanon State Forest. Used with permission.

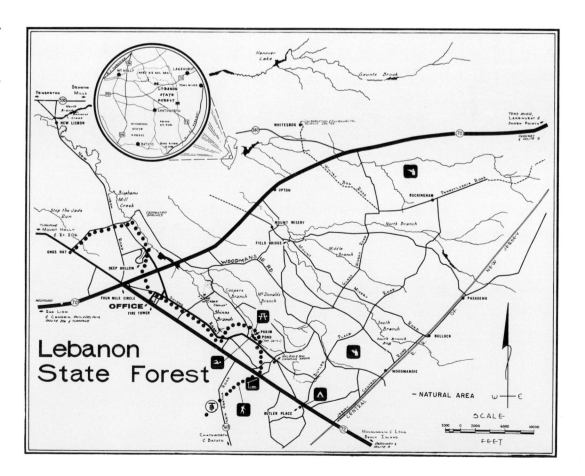

voices," as Norman put it, "the anxiousness of them." (Interview, Jan. 22, 1986)

Smoke, Sailor, and Nip are among Norman's best "trailers." Hunters often "cast" their trail dogs by releasing them on a road known to be in a fox's territory. In this method, called "road hunting," the truck proceeds slowly down the road, with the dogs ahead of it. The hounds busily look for the sign of fox, inspecting tufts of broomsedge, pine needles, and Indian grass, pausing occasionally to void themselves, depositing their own scent on top of all others. The air is filled with the sound of long ears flapping vigorously, a motion that hunters say helps to stir up the scent. Their tails tick slightly in excitement as various animal scents arouse their interest, but if no scent of fox emerges, "no action," as Milton Collins put it, they remain mute, straining to isolate fox pheromones in a world crowded with aroma. "Did you know," Norman reflected, "a dog's nose must be something out of this world":

Because you have to specifically smell the difference between a fox, a rabbit, a deer— and yet, they get to the point where I've seen hounds that would run red fox and wouldn't run gray, and vice-versa. Now their nose is that keen that they can tell the difference between a red fox and a gray fox. (Foxchase, Jan. 25, 1986)

Without seeing it, foxhunters can tell a fox's running pattern by the way the hounds sound, and a fox tells them by the way it runs whether it is red (*Vulpes fulva*) or gray (*Urocyon cinereoargenteus*). They offer radically different chases.

The red fox, model for Reynard, the indomitable trickster of the Medieval animal world, is the flashier creature. Far fleeter of foot than either gray foxes or dogs, it prefers open running and will lead the dogs for miles down fire lanes, railroads, and across open fields. It also gives off a stronger scent than a gray fox, enabling the hounds to run faster, harder, and louder. Some wildlife biologists say the red fox was introduced by English colonists in the eighteenth century for the sake of the sport.[3]

Norman remembers that red foxes first made their appearance in Lebanon State Forest in the 1940s. One of the earliest and most memorable was a fox they named

Norman Taylor watching Bo and Blue in conference at a scent post. Photograph by Dennis McDonald, January 1989

Fireball. "He would let you run him," Norman recalled:

He was a nice fox. He liked to be run. . . . I seen him stand on the road, after you catch dogs, and watch you when you're tired out. When the dogs are tired right out, he'd stand down the road and watch you load your dogs. . . . just laughin' at us. (Interview, Nov. 28, 1980)

While red foxes run straight through open areas for miles, gray foxes circle, and cling to the brush and briars. "He keeps you in heavy cover all the time," said Norman.

Because the hunting area is becoming more congested with traffic, and because of competing noises from air traffic, chain saws, recreational vehicles, and military testing, Pine Barrens foxhunters sometimes prefer the gray foxes that circle, that keep the dogs in hearing distance, away from the dangers of major highways. "The gray fox'll run a closer area," said Norman, "and give us more chance to get in around him." (Foxchase, Jan. 25, 1986)

Also known as a "ringing fox" because of its running pattern, the gray fox signals that "it has had enough" when it begins "doubling back" continuously. Then the hunters will "break" the dogs, driving their trucks to a point where the fox is apt to cross. Catching the fox is not their aim, for, within their lifetimes, the fox has gone from being despised as vermin to being prized as a conductor of canine symphonies. Most foxhunters have abandoned the practice of shooting foxes after running them for hours because the destruction of fox habitat has depleted fox populations in the region. Since the dogs could kill the fox if they caught it, hunters call them off the chase at the first sign of fox fatigue. "There's no sense of catchin' him," Norman said, "because once he's caught, you're done with that fox forever." (Interview, Jan. 22, 1986)

While his trail dogs tongue the cold trail, Norman Taylor listens with his runners for the sound of the hot track. Photograph by Dennis McDonald, January 1989

Until the dogs find a track, they are guided by the truck, a surrogate "alpha" hound with its own distinctive rallying cry. It is not the sound of the classic, brass hunter's horn, curved and tassled, but the horn beneath the hood of a given truck that these foxhounds respond to. Norman has a special horn installed for this purpose. It gives out a high "Hwah!" of a honk, in contrast to the more restrained tenor toot that comes from Horsetrader's Chevrolet pickup. Leon Hopkins, known to fox-hunters as Horsetrader, has had that horn on three different trucks.

Sometimes the hunter himself guides the hounds on foot away from the road, down a deer path toward the swamp, encouraging them. "Hark up!" says Norman. "Hark on it, Smoke!" "Go on 'im, Nip!" "Spring to 'im, Sailor!"

This morning the action is brewing over by Reeves's Bogs, where Horsetrader has found a hot track.

The CB radio sputters and Horsetrader says, "You got a copy of me, Dogman? How 'boutcha Yellow Bird, you got a copy of me?"

Yellow Bird grabs the mike and says, "Yeah, I got a copy of you."

"My dogs are running. I'm crossin' the blacktop here and goin' to the Muddy Road," Horsetrader informs him.

"All righty," says Yellow Bird. "We'll pick some dogs up and come over."

Leon Hopkins has foxhunted for nearly seven decades. He traded fox dogs with Norman's father. His hat, a gift from his son-in-law, has a reclining fox on it, hand-painted by a neighbor. Leon's handle, Horsetrader, alludes to the forty horses he boards on his farm in Cookstown near McGuire Air Force Base, and the dozens more he is usually buying, selling, and trading. Because of his emphysema he depends on an inhalator, and his wife, Betty, often joins him on foxchases, to help him load and unload his dogs.

While Horsetrader keeps his ear on the action, Dogman and Yellow Bird summon their dogs from the cold trails.

Norman pushes his way into the swamp, about fifty yards from the road, and calls to his dogs, using a coarse "Heeyah!" and a "Whoop!" Hunters have an assortment of vocal calls for collecting their dogs, ranging from the more gutteral "Eeyah! Eeyah! Hah! Hah! Hah! Hah!" to a shrill "Whoo!" But each dog knows the voice of its master, just as it knows the horn of the master's truck.

When he has loaded his six trailers, adding them to the eight in his truck, Norman starts the engine and sets off at a terrific speed for his destination, the fox's projected crossing place, about a mile and a half away.

In contrast to the hounds, foxhunters follow the chase prospectively, predicting where a given fox will lead the hounds so they can watch them cross the roads. For this task it is the pickup truck, not the horse, that is the perfect vehicle for riding to hounds in the Pine Barrens, for circumnavigating fox chases on narrow sand roads, overhung with pine boughs. They take the CB antennae into the cab for these forays, during which one is all but deafened by the sound of pine branches slapping and scraping against the sides of the truck.

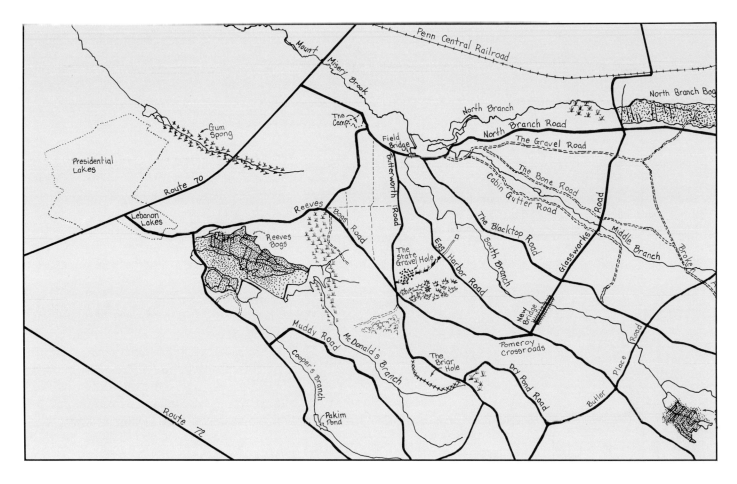

Map labels: Penn Central Railroad, Mount Misery Brook, North Branch, North Branch Road, North Branch Bog, The Camp, Field Bridge, The Gravel Road, The Bone Road, Cabin Gutter Road, Gum Spong, Presidential Lakes, Route 70, Reeves Boss Road, Butterworth Road, The State Gravel Hole, Egg Harbor Road, The Blacktop Road, South Branch, Glassworks Road, Middle Branch, Broken, Lebanon Lakes, Reeves Bogs, New Bridge, Muddy Road, McDonald's Branch, Cooper's Branch, The Briar Hole, Pomeroy Crossroads, Dry Pond Road, Butler Place Road, Route 72, Pakim Pond

The world of foxchasing in Lebanon State Forest. "Everybody that comes up in the woods has got their own names for the roads," said Donald Taylor. Drawing by Donald Shomette and Kevin Hodges based on a field sketch by Mary Hufford

There are only a few paved roads through the forest, referred to by foxhunters as "blacktops," and only local people can travel with assurance the unpaved labyrinth from Chatsworth to Browns Mills, on routes that were established well before Routes 70 and 72 became major routes to the Jersey shore. The passable roads circumscribe "pieces of woods" inlaid with miles and miles of one-lane sand roads, crossways, and dams, artifacts of the region's nineteenth-century industrial heyday, made by charcoalers, lumbermen, and cranberry growers. More recently, some were made by foxhunters.

In contrast to most of the forest's urban visitors, foxhunters know the landscapes as only people who worked them can know them. Though they have worked at jobs outside of the forest, Norman Taylor, Junie Bell, and Leon Hopkins think of themselves first as woodsmen. Within their lifetimes, however, the woods have gone from private ownership to public ownership. The swamps in the forest have gone from being work places to recreational and scientific landscapes. Where once farmers welcomed the canine chorus, newcomers complain about it. Foxes have gone from being "outlaws," as Leon Hopkins put it, to valued beasts of the chase, and the woods, formerly devoid of deer, are now full of them.

And the roads have been improved. In foxhunters' parlance, unpaved but improved roads include "tar roads," "gravel roads," and "dirt roads."

"When they put those gravel roads in, they ruined Lebanon State Forest," complained Norman. "They do to all forests, because that lets everybody in. Everybody with a car can ride up and down them good roads."

But not everyone with a car can enter the foxhunters' world. John Earlin, who foxhunted for nearly seven decades before his death in 1986, made this point in a story he told when I first met him. "A man pulled up here in a pink Cadillac one night," he began:

About two o'clock in the morning, and wanted to know what I was doin' out here

at that hour. "Well," I said, "you roll down your window, mister, and you'll hear some of the prettiest music you ever heard in your life." So the guy rolled down his window and listened. After a bit he said, "How can you hear any music when those dogs are making all that racket?" (Foxchase, Nov. 15, 1980)

Norman pulls up to the blacktop where Leon's pickup is parked. Leon's dogs have crossed and are making a racket. Norman stops and his hounds, some of them younger and still learning "what their noses are for," hear Leon's dogs from the box and grow frantic with desire to join the chase. Norman lets his more experienced dogs out first, the ones that can "locate."

Once Sailor, a methodical hound, has found and verified the track, Norman opens the box, and the others pour forth, a stream of brown, black, and white, of scrambled ears, noses, legs, tails, and ribs, issuing forth in a single canine rush, each hound siphoning out the one behind it. Crying out eagerly to the dogs ahead of them, they disappear into the brush.

"That's all they know is gettin' in there," says Norman.

Having started the fox, hounds on the "hot track" begin to "chop," flooding the air with staccato notes. They are no longer trailing but running. Another foxchase has materialized, a dynamic fusion of landscape, animals, and hunters.

Each foxchase is an enactment, a story, as the hunters put it. "Chasin' a fox," said Norman, "is about like tellin' a story. Only the dogs are tellin' it to you":

It's like they talk to each other. When you hear one start right up sharp, he's hollering, "Here I am! I got it! I got it!" You can tell, yeah. Like different dogs say, "I got it! I got it! I got it!" And you hear 'em all come at him and get in with him, yeah. (Interview, Jan. 24, 1986)

The single roar, produced by all the hounds running in a pack together, helps consolidate the hunters at the edge, united by the sound and their shared understanding of it.[4] In the human group, members who playfully bear animal names listen to storytellers in an animal pack, whose members

are named for people. It is a story of epic
proportions, told over and over by Maggie,
Becky, Lil, Sailor, Maude, Jake, Mike,
Dave, Smiley, and Kate to an appreciative
audience comprised of Yellow Bird, Dogman, Piggy, Green Fox, Blowfish, Mustang,
Horsetrader, Redbone, Blue Tick, Gray
Fox, and others in the community—a community defined by the capacity of its members to listen and hear it as music, a
community whose aliases catch up the
landscape's animals and hues.

In the United States there are two major
traditions of foxhunting. The more famous
tradition is English-style, or formal, foxhunting, in which the participants,
mounted on half-bred horses (called "hunters"), "ride to" pedigreed hounds. Less well
known is the informal tradition of "listening to hounds," which goes by a variety of
regional names, such as "hilltopping,"
"ridge-running," "forks-of-the-creek," and
"one-gallus" (that is, "one-suspender")
foxhunting.

While the formal hunters ride to the
hounds in a display of horsemanship, the
informal hunters listen to the hounds as
part of an exercise in dogmanship. The
practitioners link these differences with
deeper distinctions in social class. Jack Davis, a foxhunter from Browns Mills, New
Jersey, distinguished Pine Barrens foxhunters from the "tally-hos" saying: "They're
the upper class, and we're the lower class."
Formal foxhunters, according to a well-
known anecdote, distinguish themselves by
the language that gave them their nick-
name: "We say 'Tally-ho,' not 'There goes
the son-of-a-bitch.'"[5]

Formal foxhunting celebrates social hierarchy in every aspect of language, costume,
and procession. "It's a very class-oriented
situation," a young woman who rides with
the Monmouth Hunt Club told me. "It's the
hierarchy."

You ride in sections: first comes the master
of the hunt, then the whipper-in and the
mistress of the hunt—and they are, as we
used to say, "God Almighty in red." You
must wear your uniform, and it's a wonder-
ful thing. It's class—you are a gentleman
and a lady at all times, and you wear your

proper habit, and your horse is properly rigged. Jacqueline *Kennedy* got thrown out of a hunt club once for showing up in her own hunt colors. (Interview, Nov. 20, 1980)

Informal hunting lacks a rigorously enforced dress code, though men outfit themselves according to an unspoken agreement that approves sensible boots, baggy trousers, and a warm jacket, topped off by a cap. Most of them also sport some form of insignia, usually a fox or a hound.

The relationship between hunters and dogs is structured differently in the two forms of hunting. Formal hunters, preoccupied with horses, do not train the hounds themselves, which are collectively owned by the club, are managed by a paid employee, and are always registered. The mounted foxhunters do not compete via the dogs, but via displays of equestrian skill and nerve. Harking back to the conquering hero on horseback, they manage horses, not dogs. Hounds are more their heralds than their representatives.

In contrast, working-class hunting emphasizes the ability of individual hunters to obtain and train good fox dogs. Most importantly, the hounds are individually owned. Each hound in the chase is an extension of one of the hunters listening in the distance. Each hunter could, if necessary, conduct an entire chase with his own hounds, but, as Norman put it, "It's in competition that you find out what you've got."

None of the Pine Barrens dogs are registered, for this chase emphasizes performance over pedigree. "A dog can be the ugliest dog in the world," as Donald Pomoroy put it, "so long as he can go in there and do his job." A debate over the concept of nobility is implied in both settings. Anthropologist James Howe argues that, for the upper-class hunter:

The chase is concerned with a tension or contradiction between ascription and achievement that is common to hereditary aristocracies. While upper-class ideologies stress that social class is a matter of birth and thus unchanging, at the same time they wish to promote the idea that the accomplishments and behavior of the upper classes justify their position and that they deserve to be where they are. . . . Such displays advance the proposition that the two senses of the word "nobility" are synonymous.[6]

However, for working-class foxhunters the two senses of the word are not synonymous. The message for upper-class foxhunters reads: "By virtue of our birth we are noble, and our behavior illustrates this." For working-class foxhunters it reads: "Birth has nothing to do with it." In this way the two forms coexist as opposing terms in an argument, constructed around the same inner event of a pack of hounds in noisy pursuit of a fox.

"You meet a good class of people foxhuntin'," said Norman once. "I don't care what anybody says."

The stressing of network over hierarchy is partly reflected in the system of naming whereby Pine Barrens hunters keep track of scores of unregistered hounds. In the poetics of hound naming, we find an ad hoc index to hound genealogies. Thus Randall Stafford named three sibling pups Coffee, Tea, and Cocoa; Donald Pomoroy named a pair Left and Right; and Robly Champion had three consecutive pairs named Slip and Slide, names that allude alliteratively to hound movements in chases, as well as to their blood relationships. Norman paired two siblings born in 1985 as Halley and Comet. Other pairs include Nip and Tuck, Jack and Jenny, and Punch and Judy.

"Things like that keep the litters in mind," he explained. (Interview, Jan. 24, 1986)

Often the names become by extension an index to the hunting community, linking pups with the men who bred them. Joe Albert purchased a pair of puppies from a man afflicted with shingles and named them Shingles and Jingles. Donald Pomoroy's Freeman came from Freeman Taylor, and Jack Davis's Jake came from Jake Meredith. Norman Taylor's Snap, Chunk, and Bull were nicknames of Randall Stafford, his wife, and his brother. "And, Johnny Earlin named one Norman every now and then," Norman explained. (Interview, Jan. 24, 1986)

As sociable beings, foxhounds and foxes are polar opposites. Animal ethologists, arranging canids along a spectrum from the least sociable to the most sociable, classify the fox as a Type I canid, the sort that does not mate for life, a competitive, noncooperative hunter. A solitary hunter, it stalks smaller game by stealth and ambush. Wolves, wild progenitors of domestic dogs, are Type III canids. They hunt openly and in large, socially stratified packs, bringing down quarry larger than themselves.

The chase, then, actually reverses the natural order of things. The wild pack evolved in order to hunt cooperatively for game that was larger than individuals in the pack; game that could provide a meal for the entire pack, game like bison or the deer that hounds lose their jobs for pursuing. While it is not quite natural for wolves to hunt small creatures as a pack, foxhunting is based in part on the suppression of such instincts in dogs, on the triumph of cultivation over natural impulses. Social stratification is also structured out of the domestic pack in a variety of ways.

The olfactory and vocal messages of foxes and hounds relate to their status as sociable beings. Michael Fox, a canine ethologist, points out that collective "singing," the hallmark of sociable canids, "may serve some positive socially cohesive function for the group" and "may also serve a territorial function, informing other groups of their presence." [7]

Similarly, the unsociable canid's disagreeable odor is thought to maintain territory and social distance. Fox observes that "an interesting inverse correlation is found between the intensity of body odours, especially of the tail and anal glands, and the degree of sociability in canids." [8] Glands at the base of the fox's long, bushy tail account for a distinctive "foxy" odor not possessed by wolves or dogs. They also account for the red fox's medieval moniker: "beast of the stinking chase."

"If he gets runnin' hard," said Norman, "you can smell him, and a red fox more 'n a gray. And if anything, he smells skunky. Yeah, smells just like a skunk." (Foxchase, Jan. 25, 1986)

In foxhunting, then, we see the most sociable canid pitted against the least sociable, not for food, but ostensibly to take vocal charge of the territory the fox has claimed with its scent. And while sociable beings drive out an unsociable being at the center of the hunt, the hunters dispel unsociability with sociable talk at the edge. "That's what it's all about," said Norman. "Good fellowship, where you can kid and nobody gets mad at each other." (Foxchase, Jan. 25, 1986)

The hounds, of course, disregard the "keep out" aspect of the fox's message, and on "striking the line" issue a call to assembly, a canine chorus that is called "singing" by hunters and animal ethologists alike. Through their singing, the hounds take over the territory marked by the fox, conveying it to the hunters. The fox, an "outsider" canid, does not respond to the singing as music, any more than human outsiders do. And, bound by no code of honor, the fox, through concealing and distorting its trail, does what it can to suppress the music. [9]

As we listen, the voices dwindle, bobbing away in the distance. Horsetrader and Dogman have strategically placed themselves where the chase might emerge on the far side of the "piece of woods." Others have joined us here, lengthening the caravan of parked pickups, and swelling the group of listeners. Donald Taylor is here with his son, Greg, and his father, Harry, who is Norman's older brother. Norman's cousin, Hank Stevenson, is here and so is Norman's wife, Caroline, whose CB handle is Cranberry Lady. She came late, bearing Fig Newtons and hot water for tea and coffee.

"If it's not a gray fox, I would be surprised, really," says Norman.

"If he was a red, he'd a been over North Branch by this time," Hank Stevenson agrees.

"He'll be back here," Norman predicts.

A burst of static from the CB and a voice says, "Tally-ho!"

"Who said 'Tally-ho'?" I ask.

"Junie, because he seen the fox," says Norman. " 'Tally-ho!' means you see him."

It was a gray fox, as Norman predicted.

At the edge the hunters try to hear the fox's trail as the hounds take possession of it. The hounds must therefore follow the trail on the ground, not the scent on the wind. The narrowness of the trail forces the hounds to "bunch up" or "pack together." They should "bunch up" so tightly that, as Norman's brother Freeman put it, "you could throw a blanket over them."

The hound in the lead may be said to "own the line." This line is a raw material that hounds transform into an expressive medium. Each hound has its own style of expressing the trail, and something of a hound's character is revealed in its style of running. Comparing the process to a craft, Norman distinguishes his hounds according to whether they run "neat" or "clean"; whether they "swing," "cut," "hunt 'em wide," or tend to "boo-hoo."

"There's the kind of hound that boo-hoos," Norman explained. "They just get a track and they can't move it." (Interview, Jan. 22, 1986) Norman recalled how his favorite hound, Lead, made the trail come alive:

When the smellin' got right that he could run fast, he was fast, and when it was bad, you could see him—like a snake, he'd wiggle it. (Interview, Jan. 24, 1986)

And Leon Hopkins's Maeve has a distinctive way of striking a line:

She's got a funny way. When she hits a trail she rares up on her back legs and barks right up in the air, when she first hits, yeah. It's comical to watch her. If she struck out here in the road she'd rare up right up in the air and bark, and then put her nose back down again and then go. (Foxchase, Jan. 22, 1986)

Hounds are expected to strike a balance between cooperation and competition. The hounds are supposed to be so compatible that no one hound is consistently in the lead or in the rear—they are expected to "honor" the dog that has the scent.

At one end of the scale are hounds that pretend to have the scent, the "babblers" and "trashers." These develop reputations among the other dogs. "They know," said Norman. "If you got a dog that gets noisy, that's babblin' noisy, and just not—tongue where it belongs to be—dogs learn that dog and they won't honor it, yeah." (Foxchase, Jan. 25, 1986)

A caravan of pickups on the blacktop. "Most of the people around here just like to hear the dogs run," said Donald Taylor. "You just hang around for a half-hour listening to the dogs, and then you move on about your own business." Photograph by Dennis McDonald, January 1989

At the other end are the cheaters. "Your best dog isn't always in the front," said John Earlin:

If one dog is always in the front, he is cheating somehow or other. That type of dog we don't particularly like: one that cheats, because it takes the music outa our pack. In other words, say they're runnin' out here and the dog come out here and run down the road and grab the fox, he, to me, is of no value. (Interview, Nov. 15, 1980)

The prescriptive canons for hound interaction minimize hierarchy and echo the canons for pure sociability among humans. Sociologist Georg Simmel observed that the classic expression of human sociability is talk for its own sake, wherein "the individual shall not present his peculiarities and individuality with too much abandon and aggressiveness." [10]

Hunters fashion foxchases in part around the fox's ability to fabricate, that is, to construct what Erving Goffman calls "a plot or treacherous plan leading—when realized—to a falsification of some part of the world." [11] The part of the world the fox falsifies is its own trail. The fox can lead dogs to think it has crossed the road when it has in fact come to the road and doubled back on its trail, or that it has doubled back, following a previous pattern, when in fact it has gone up a tree. The basic fabrication consists of making hounds think the trail is not where it is, of hiding the trail or disguising its direction. Jack Davis marveled at a fox that ran a railroad track in the snow, and slipped only once, leaving one footprint. One footprint, of course, is not a trail.

"Foxes aren't called foxes just for the name," said Jack Davis. "They're foxy."

"You talk about foxes bein' foxy," said Ann Davis, his wife, who also hunted. "If they think they're gettin' closed in they'll run right down the middle of the road. Not down the *ruts,* down the *middle*—where fumes from the car, oils and things, you know, the dogs can't trail 'em." (Interview, Nov. 21, 1980)

Foxes have even been known to stop abruptly and let a pack of dogs rush over them, giving themselves a good lead in the opposite direction before hounds get wise to the ploy.

Of a fox on another occasion Norman said, "I seen him skulkin'—where he'd try to run right back through the dogs. . . . You can see 'im skulk, and the dogs shut up. . . . Sooner or later some dog's gonna catch sight of him." (Interview, Oct. 17, 1986)

On this occasion the fox has already tricked the dogs several times, emerging at the blacktop and running up it in order to "outfox the dogs," as Hank Stevenson put it. Thus it buys time for itself as the dogs scatter to frantically sniff out its point of entry back into the brush. The hound that finds the line again is a bit of a hero. "When they almost missed that fox there," said Norman, replaying one scene,

Sailor threw out just wide enough to get on it where no dogs had been on it. And I said, "Boy, they better hark if they're gonna get with him," and sure enough, they all harked, and that was it. Soon as he hollered, I knew he was right, 'cause he never hollers unless he's right. Nope. He's a hunter. (Foxchase, Jan. 25, 1986)

Norman Taylor and Ted Goff listen from New Bridge to hounds chasing the fox through South Branch. "It's a sound that carries the foxhounds," said Norman Taylor. "I love to hear 'em run in the cedar." Photograph by Dennis McDonald, January 1989

When it cannot mystify, the fox ensnares, eking out more lead for itself by taking the hounds through treacherous briars or "laps"—swamps full of wind-thrown cedar and slash from lumbering operations. "They're briarin' in there," says Norman, listening. "If you had a bird's-eye view, he's crawlin' right underneath the briars—that's why you don't get no noise outa the dogs. He's right underneath them briars. He's skinnier 'n a rabbit dog." (Foxchase, Jan. 25, 1986)

Each foxchase spreads a temporary soundscape over the spaces in Lebanon State Forest. Whereas formal foxhunters exert dominion over rolling countrysides by riding over them, informal hunters capture the land in a net of sound.

The landscapes of Lebanon State Forest are in fact partially recast in terms of what the fox can do with them. Foxes can tire dogs out on the Plains, say foxhunters, by keeping them away from water. They can use the plowed lanes and narrow fire lines to string out the hounds and dilute the music. Control burning, done by the Forest Fire Service in February and March to eliminate brush that lets fires get out of control, leaves a charred landscape that overpowers scent, and that foxes can use to foil the dogs. In cold weather, bogs, ponds, and swamps may turn to ice that foxes scamper across but that dogs negotiate with difficulty. Thus foxchases change with the passing seasons to produce landscape habits uniquely witnessed by foxhunters. "Everyday it's different," said Norman.

Foxhunters impose on the forest a set of meanings and landscape categories related to foxhunting. For foxhunters, the sport opens the fixed quantity of land within the borders of the state forest out to a limitless array of possibilities. The forest becomes, in Einstein's terms, "bounded but infinite."

The forest of the foxhunters is a hidden world, wedged in among countless others, as Werner Sombart reminds us:

No "forest" exists as an objectively prescribed environment. There exists only forester-, hunter-, botanist-, walker-, nature enthusiast-, woodgatherer-, berry picker- and a fairytale-forest in which Hansel and Gretel lose their way.[12]

The Lebanon State Forest of foxhunters is a world they have chased and uttered into being, a world made of language and memory that impinges on the worlds of others through the ephemeral soundscapes established by the canine chorus. It jockeys for position alongside the worlds of deerhunters, dogsledders, recreational vehicle users, hikers, campers, scientists, and growers who lease cranberry bogs from the state.

Foxhunting provides an alternative way of looking at landscape features that went unnoticed in the forest-as-workplace. Various landscape features burnt ground, tar roads, plowed lanes—are understood in terms of how well they support or impede the chase. "Pushcover," for example, emerges as a kind of vegetation that slows dogs down in their pursuit of fox.

"He's runnin' in the swamp now," said Norman, listening from the Blacktop. "It's real heavy huckleberry and ganderbrush swamp, yeah."

"What other kinds of swamp are there?" I ask.

"There's open swamps like your gum swamps and whatnot, but this is all heavy pushcover—where dogs have to just push through it." (Foxchase, Jan. 25, 1986)

The hunters, listening to the canine nucleus galloping over the many surfaces of the forest, listening until their ears become their eyes, strive to achieve consensus on the exact location of the chase. They bring the implied narrative to completion in human terms, giving form in language to the images of the chase and the landscape that condenses out of the sound before their minds' eyes.

We stand in the road, facing a solid wall of pine trees, a filter for canine voices. Beyond them we can see the tops of cedars.

"They're right in the cedar swamp," said Norman, translating hound voices into vision. "Lot of water. Yeah, and if it was frozen up in there in the ice, you couldn't run that fox in there could you?"

"No," says Leon.

"Nope," Norman continues. "Right where they're at now, beavers have made a dam in there. It goes right around and if it was froze up, you wouldn't hear no music at all."

"With that much water on top of the ice, that has trouble too," Leon elaborates. "They *walk* through it, you know. The fox does, and the dogs."

"Leaves no scent where he goes through on top of the ice," adds Norman, "and there's water on top of it." (Interview, Jan. 25, 1986)

But cedar swamps, while difficult for dogs to negotiate because of "laps" (windthrown cedar) and "hassocks" (cedar root formations overgrown with sphagnum moss), are acoustically magnificent.

The gray fox's course through the forest landscape. Landscape features are like a hand of cards dealt to the fox, who is depicted as manipulating them aggressively to increase its lead and suppress its scent. "He won't go out in these oaks," said Norman Taylor of a gray fox. "He doesn't have lead enough to go out in these oaks." A briar patch is the gray fox's trump card. "That's the thing your gray fox does," said Jack Davis. "He likes to take you in the briars." Drawing by Donald Shomette and Kevin Hodges based on a field sketch by Mary Hufford

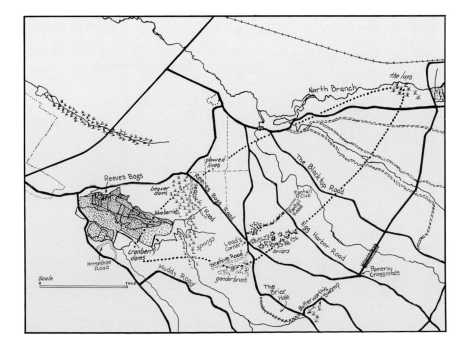

"It's a sound that carries the foxhounds," said Norman, one time in conversation with Junie and Leon. "I love to hear 'em run in the cedar. Don't you?"

"Butterworth Crossway is a good spot," affirmed Junie. "When they're comin' through that swamp there, that's just a roar."

"There to the crossway," Leon reiterated, "boy, they roar in there." (Interview, Oct. 18, 1986)

According to Christian Bethman, the Pine Barrens have the second-highest incidence of forest fires in the country. Fires have made aspects of the landscape ephemeral and are constantly erasing the kinds of landscape artifacts that elsewhere preserve communal memories, like old homesteads, historic mills, and hunting cabins.

But hound voices are a phenomenon that fires cannot destroy. The languages of hounds and foxes do not change over time or space as do the languages of humans. In 1940 Charles Grant of New Egypt told a tall tale to folklorist Herbert Halpert that in a way celebrates the triumph of voices over ephemerality. In his fabrication the voices literally become an artifact hovering over the landscape:

[Ed Leek] went down there fox huntin'. Said he stood up there on the Hundred Dollar Bridge Hill we called it, and, uh, he heared his dogs runnin' a fox, comin' right towards him. An' he said he stood there an hour and they didn't get no closer, and they were only half a mile from him when he heard them an' they didn't get no closer. He said he started to go in there where they was, and see what was the matter—he got excited about it. An' he found their tracks on an old sand road where they'd scratched and gone by, and they'd gone by 'fore he got there. It was so cold it froze their voice up in the air, and they stayed right there. The voice stayed there and didn't leave. There was the string of their voice for a mile long, an' that stayed there after the dogs gone by. Their yells stayed there; kept right on yellin'. The cold ketched it up in the air and never let it go—till it thawed out next spring some time, when it got warm.[13]

Hounds' voices animate landscape features saturated with personal memories and meanings. Foxes and hounds career over the landscapes, roaring out their images, lighting up scenes that were long ago emblazoned in the mind. The foxchase loosens nuggets of memory that, like cranberries, dislodged from vines by mechanical wet harvesters, pop to the surface.

Hank is reminded of something that happened not far from where the dogs are running. "Remember about thirty years ago when you had that fox treed right there on the upper end of that reservoir?"

Norman does not, exactly.

Hank persists. "You don't remember that? You and I and Herb Anderson was in there."

Norman helps him paint the picture. "One time I had a couple good tree dogs, and if the gray fox run up a tree, they stayed right there and barked, yeah. Those two dogs had every dog barkin'. But now if you tree a fox you'll probably—it's just the end of your chase."

"Never know it," avers Hank.

"It's just a matter of havin' a good tree dog, yeah," says Norman, bragging a little. "I've treed a lot of foxes when my dogs was runnin' 'em."

"When we got in there that day, the fox was in the tree," Hank reiterates.

"Up the tree, yeah," Norman picks up, "I had Jacky then, probably. A dog called Jacky. A blue dog, and, man, he was the best tree dog I ever saw in my life. He could tree a fox. Sat right there and had all the dogs around treein'."

Hank starts the reprise. "Well, you and I and Herb Anderson went in there that day."

"Yeah, how about that," Norman muses.

"That's been a while ago," says Hank. "Yeah, a few moons's went by."

Norman brings them back to the present, reorienting them. "I can just [i.e. barely] hear 'em," he says. "They went off that way."

Placemaking is a human territorial behavior. Foxchases tease places out of seem-

Snapshot of hounds treeing a gray fox, ca. 1935. "Gray foxes don't go in a hole like a red fox," said Norman Taylor. "You get him tired out, he'll go in a hole. He knows where all the holes are. He'll get in one. Now a gray fox'll climb a tree . . . . He'll climb right up it, just like a cat if you get runnin' him too hard." From the family album of Randall Stafford

ingly undifferentiated woodlands. Place names are chaseworld remnants—flags whereby hunters lay claim to contested portions of Lebanon State Forest.

Names for places to cast hounds include "Chicken Line," "Feeding Pile," and "Bone Road," where hunters put out food to attract foxes. Such places are marked with what Chris Bethmann interpreted as foxhunter sign. "This is one of the sure sign that there were foxhunters around," he said, pointing to a pile of bones near the Goose Pond, "the bones from cattle or horses or whatever they can get their hands on."

"What do they do with them?" I asked.

"Well, they'll dump piles of bones like that, with meat still on 'em," he explained:

That will attract the fox, and that'll give them someplace to start their dogs from, because they'll know that the fox'll be there after dark, gnawin' away on those bones. They'll release their dogs around this area and let them scare the fox up and they're off and running. Sometimes you'll find just piles and piles and piles of bones. (Interview, Sept. 16, 1983)

Names for places where foxes routinely lose dogs include "the Bad Place," "the Briar Hole," and "the Featherbeds," a quaking bog near Chatsworth. And a place called "Underwear" came into being around the capture of a fox, according to Joe Albert:

There was a place over in Warren Grove, and I went over there one time to hear guys' dogs, you know, and I said, "Damn if I ain't comin' over here some night." And I went

over, and the first night I went there, they caught the fox, and I pulled a bush down on the cranberry bogs, and I hung a note. And there was a pair of winter underwear hangin' on this road where I caught it, you know. The guy musta got warm, and he took 'em off and hung 'em up. And I put, "Caught fox by underwear," you know. And the guys laughed. They told me that so many times. They caught fox by under wear. (Interview, Aug. 12, 1982)

Such spaces, once distinguished, become important reference points in human conversation.

"So you call that area 'Underwear' now?" I asked.

"Yeah," said Joe Albert. "After that they'd tell ya, they'd say, 'We was right where the underwear was. We was runnin' one,' you know." (Interview, Aug. 12, 1982)

Burial places for particular hounds also serve as reference points, places like "Spike's Field" and "Lead's Corner."

"He's buried," said Milton Collins, of a favorite hound named Spike, "where a fox crosses his grave."

The burial place of Lead, the best fox dog that Norman Taylor ever owned, is on the edge of Butterworth Crossway. "I've got all hopes of being buried there," said Norman, "being cremated and buried in the same place." (Interview, Jan. 22, 1986)

My brother and I, we worked all day to bury 'im. It was one of the saddest days of our life, I think. And we buried 'im here in Lebanon State Forest where he run his first fox. And, any foxhunter that goes by knows where it's at, and they always say, "Old Lead's buried there." (Interview, Jan. 22, 1986)

There are also commemorative sites for deceased hunters: These are marked with signs in an effort to spread the use of the names beyond the hunting community, allowing the world of the chase to leak into the realms of others. At the intersection officially known as Five Corners a handsome stone marker renames the intersection "Pomoroy's Crossroads" in honor of Donald Pomoroy. Below the lettering a foxhound is engraved in pursuit of a fox.

"Believe it or not," said Norman Taylor,

Breaking the hounds from the fox's trail, Norman Taylor ushers them out of the chase and into the dog box. "We never kill a fox, we protect him," said Taylor. "There's no sense of catchin' him, because once he's caught, you're done with that fox forever." Photograph by Dennis McDonald, January 1989

"By puttin' the sign there, people will see it, and they'll start usin' that name. Pomoroy's Corners, yeah, and that's how it'll get established." (Foxchase, Jan. 25, 1986)

Pomoroy was killed late in 1985 when his pickup truck went out of control and crashed into a tree. The truck was green, and because of that his CB name was Green Fox. Hunters always heard him before they saw him, entering the circle of fellowship voice first. "You could hear him every morning comin' in," said Norman. "You could tell how far away he was. You could tell when he was gettin' closer:

"Hey, who's up there who's up there? Who's in the woods? Piggy, Piggy, Piggy, where are you? Dogman, Dogman, I can't hear you." He'd like sing all the way down to you. Then he'd say, "Yel-low B-ird!" Like he was singing to you! Yeah, he was funny. (Interview, Jan. 24, 1986)

His funeral service was conducted at the "Rye Strips," a feeding ground for deer in Lebanon State Forest. His hounds attended the funeral as well, watching quietly from the dog box in a pickup truck. Pomoroy's wife, Patsy, distributed them among his foxhunting buddies afterward: four to Yellow Bird, four to Dogman, and three to Piggy.

The gray fox has circled now for six hours, crossing Reeves's Bogs and the State Gravel Hole a number of times on its trek from Muddy Road to South Branch and back. He's run in the blueberries, the swamps, the spongs (lowlands where sphagnum moss grows), around the cranberry bogs and through the briars. He has "shown himself" to hunters a half-dozen times or more. His circles are tightening, a sign to foxhunters that it is time to break the dogs.

The trucks are lined up on Egg Harbor Road. The hunters are poised, several with long leather bullwhips they grip more firmly when the fox emerges from the woods and races down the road about fifteen yards before the woods on the other

Sorting the hounds following the chaotic break-up of the chase, Norman Taylor, Jim Giglio, and Harvey Baker, Jr., ensure that all hounds are present and accounted for. Photographs by Dennis McDonald, January 1989

side close behind him. The onrushing dogs, a minute behind him, are getting louder. As those in the lead explode out of the brush, hunters begin tooting horns, whooping, and cracking whips against the road, as if to sever the impalpable line of scent and concentration that binds hounds to the fox. The world of the chase is shattered, and the dogs begin to mill around, climbing into the nearest dog boxes.

"Get in that truck!" shouts Norman, harshly. "Get up in there! Smoke! You know better than to go by me! Get up, Sailor! Get up, Smoke! Watch that dog, Junie! Jimmy, get in that truck! Get in that truck, Punch!"

Sometimes, if a fox is tired enough, the hunters say they can catch it first, and put it in the cab long enough for it to catch its wind. Wilted and musky, such a fox feels just like a dishrag, Norman once said. (Interview, Nov. 23, 1980)

The dogs are broken but not sorted. The hunters pull their trucks together in a clearing and raise the hinged lids of the dog boxes. Junie has Norman's Becky, and Norman has several of Junie's.

"Junie, don't let her go," says Norman. "That's Becky. If I lose Becky I'd cry. . . . Man, they're wet! They've been in the water." His voice is gentle now, not harsh, as it is when controlling dogs out of the box or kennel. "Doggy! Hello there Maggie! Here Maggie, here Maggie. There's one of yours, Junie. Another one of yours, Junie. Another one of yours, Junie."

The mighty instrument that made the soundscapes has been dismantled, its components restored to their boxes. Their hounds gathered in, the hunters begin taking leave of each other and Lebanon State Forest, repairing to the kennels and homes of everyday life.

This last separation occurs gradually. The hounds are silent now, but the air is alive with the voices of hunters. It is midnight, an old midnight several years ago. Yellow Bird, Green Fox, Blowfish, and Dogman have loaded the dogs and are parting company, each in his own truck. Their voices are the last things touching.

"You got all your dogs?" says Blowfish.

"Yeah, got all mine," returns Yellow Bird.

"About time to go the hell home then," declares Blowfish.

"Everybody got all our dogs," says Yellow Bird. "You on the tar road goin' home? Got a 10–4 on that. Good-night, I'm gonna sign off, I'm gonna shut the CB off."

"You ain't even gonna talk to me on the way home?" protests Blowfish. "I don't know about you. I don't know about you, Yellow Bird. Come on back there, ya Yellow Bird."

"How about that, Blowfish, Blowfish?" chimes in the Green Fox.

"Aw, come on back," says Blowfish, still working on Yellow Bird.

"Did you hear Green Fox?" says Green Fox, again. "You still got a Green Fox there Blowfish? Come back, ya Blowfish, Blowfish."

"Caughtcha there, Green, Green, Green Fox. Ya gotcher ears on?"

"10–4," says Green Fox. "I got 'em there, Buddy, Buddy. Where you at?"

"I'm headed for the camp," says Blowfish.

Dogman comes in. "What about you there Blowfish, do you read me?"

"I gotcha there, Dogman, Dogman," says Blowfish. "I hear you!"

But they are beginning to fade.

"10–4," says the indefatigable Blowfish, "10–4 and out."

Norman Taylor's fox-hounds, waiting for some action. Photograph by Dennis McDonald, January 1989

ACKNOWLEDGMENTS

Foxchases are exceedingly complex and difficult to capture on film and on tape. Portions of the foxchase described here appeared in the New Jersey Network video production "Pinelands Sketches." I would like to thank my colleagues and coproducers Lou Presty, Henry Sayen, and James Walsh, at New Jersey Network Public Television, for their expert documentary work, and David Steven Cohen of the New Jersey Historical Commission for collaborating on the interview of January 22, 1986.

I am also grateful to Chris Bethman, Lebanon State Forest superintendent, for help in constructing the maps.

Most of all I wish to thank the foxhunters and their families for their kindness and generous hospitality, and for opening my eyes and ears to the world of foxhunting: Norman and Caroline Taylor, Freeman Taylor, Ann Davis, Helen Earlin, Betty Hopkins, Junie and Carol Bell, Milton Collins, Robly and Gladys Champion, Donald Taylor, and Hank Stevenson. Five other foxhunters whose voices are heard in this article have passed away: Jack Davis and Donald Pomoroy in 1985; John Earlin in 1986; Joe Albert and Leon Hopkins in 1987. They are greatly missed in the Pine Barrens.

NOTES

1. This is a deviation from the standard CB scale, where "10–4" means "Roger" or "affirmative." Here it means location.

2. References to Mary Hufford's fieldnotes, journal entries, audio recordings made during foxchases, and interviews will appear in the text.

3. *See* Mary Hufford, "The Fox," in *American Wildlife in Symbol and Story,* ed. Angus Gillespie and Jay Mechling (Knoxville: University of Tennessee Press), 165–69.

4. The pack is by definition "a social group which hunts together." *See* Michael W. Fox, ed., *The Wild Canids* (New York: Van Nostrand Reinhold Company, 1975), 445.

5. Barre Toelken, personal communication.

6. James Howe, "Fox Hunting as Ritual," *American Ethnologist* 8 (1981): 29.

7. Michael W. Fox, *Behavior of Wolves, Dogs, and Related Canids* (London: Jonathan Cape, 1971), 429–30.

8. Fox, *Behavior of Wolves,* 187.

9. According to foxhunters, the gray fox is actually a member of the cat family. It makes a small, cat-like track, in contrast to the large, dog-like impression left by the red fox. Their semi-retractile front claws also enable them to climb trees, another feline trait. Moreover, one foxhunter observed that in captivity they are more prone to take to kitty litter than the red fox, and more prone to nurse from a cat. However, foxes in general are anomalous canids. For more on the feline fox phenomenon, *see* Hufford, "The Fox," 169–72.

10. Georg Simmel, *On Individuality and Social Forms,* ed. Donald Levine (Chicago: University of Chicago Press, 1971), 130.

11. Erving Goffman, *Frame Analysis* (New York: Harper Colophon Books, 1974), 83.

12. Jakob von Uexküll, *Theory of Meaning,* translated by Thure von Uexküll for special issue of *Semiotica* 42 (1982): 29.

13. Herbert Halpert, "Folktales and Legends from the New Jersey Pines: A Collection and Study," Ph.D. diss., Indiana University, 1947.

REFERENCES

Dannemann, Manuel. "Fox Hunting: A Form of Traditional Behaviour Providing Social Cohesiveness," *Folklore Studies in the Twentieth Century: Proceedings of the Centenary Conference of the Folklore Society.* London: D. S. Brewer, Rowman and Littlefield, 1980.

Emrich, Duncan. "Hound Dog Names." *Folklore on the American Land,* 141–44. Boston: Little, Brown, and Co., 1972.

Forman, Richard T. T., ed. *Pine Barrens: Ecosystem and Landscape.* New York: Academic Press, 1979.

Fox, Michael W., ed. *The Wild Canids.* New York: Van Nostrand Reinhold Company, 1975.

———., *Behavior of Wolves, Dogs and Related Canids.* London: Jonathan Cape, 1971.

Halpert, Herbert. "Folktales and Legends from the New Jersey Pines: A Collection and Study." Ph.D. diss., Indiana University, 1947.

Howe, James. "Fox Hunting as Ritual," *American Ethnologist* 8 (1981): 278–300.

Hufford, Mary. "The Fox." In *American Wildlife in Symbol and Story.* ed. Angus Gillespie and Jay Mechling. Knoxville: University of Tennessee Press, 1986.

Leach, Edmund. "Anthropological Aspects of Language: Animal Categories and Verbal Abuse." In *New Directions in the Study of Language.* ed. Eric H. Lenneberg, 23–63. Cambridge, Mass.: Massachusetts Institute of Technology Press, 1964.

———., "Ritual." *Encyclopedia of the Social Sciences,* 1968.

Lyne, David C. "What Are They Saying?: A Study of the Jargon of Hilltopping." Master's thesis, University of Kentucky, 1976.

McPhee, John. *The Pine Barrens.* New York: Farrar, Strauss, and Giroux, 1966.

Newall, Venetia J. "The Unspeakable in Pursuit of the Uneatable: Some Comments on Fox-Hunting," *Folklore* 94 (1983): 86–90.

Ortega y Gassett, Jose. *Meditations on Hunting.* New York: Charles Scribner's Sons, 1972.

Simmel, Georg. *On Individuality and Social Forms,* ed. Donald N. Levine. Chicago: University of Chicago Press, 1971.

Uexküll, Jakob von. *The Theory of Meaning,* trans. Thure von Uexküll. Special issue of *Semiotica* 42 (1982): 1–87.

Van Urk, John Blan. *The Story of American Foxhunting: From Challenge to Full Cry.* New York: Derrydale Press, 1940.

Watson, J. N. P. *The Book of Foxhunting.* New York: Arco Publishing Company, 1977.

Up on the Roof

Pigeon Flyers and City Skies

BY JANE SCHWARTZ
PHOTOGRAPHS BY TERRY HOURIGAN

On a cold autumn day, pigeon flyers Whitey Betts and Victor Ryder enjoy lunch in a little shanty they have built on their rented roof. Their birds are out "bumming," but if any "action" develops, the men will be up in an instant. Photographs for this article were taken by Terry Hourigan in 1979.

First there is a low murmur, a deep "whoo-whooing." It is followed by a slapping of wings, as if someone were shuffling a huge deck of cards overhead. Dozens of birds stream up and spiral out against the sky. A sharp whistle splits the air. A block away, a second group of birds rushes up from another rooftop; then a third group; then a fourth. Suddenly, the sky is alive with birds.

The game of pigeon flying is one of New York's least-known and most misunderstood sports. It has been taking place in full view, in public spaces, 365 days a year for over a century, yet it remains a mystery to almost all but those who play. It is an old sport, practiced primarily by working class men. Records of its existence in its present form can be traced to Europe, China, and India, and back at least four hundred years, and there are indications of a similar sport dating much earlier. Brought to New York by Italian and other European immigrants in the 1800s, the game spread rapidly throughout the city, where clusters of flat-roofed tenements provided an ideal setting for the sky-based sport.

The game has been ridiculed, scorned, or ignored by the general public, largely because of a misunderstanding about one of its central elements, the pigeon. When most people hear the word *pigeon*, they think of the common street birds—ugly, dirty scavengers, nesting anywhere, eating garbage, soiling statues, and spreading diseases. In fact, the word used by pigeon flyers when referring to these street birds is *rats*. For use in the sport, a special breed of domesticated pigeon was developed, the American Domestic Flight. Flights have nothing in common with street rats but an ancient ancestry. Flights are born and raised on the roofs in captivity and kept as clean and free of disease as any domesticated pet. Their lives are spent on the roofs, in the air, and sometimes in a pet shop, but not in the streets. Flights have several distinguishing characteristics; the most easily recognizable to an outsider is the fact that their ten primary wing tips are always white, regardless of the bird's color or other markings.

The pigeon game itself can be played with endless variations, but the essential competition goes like this: The pigeon flyer shoos his pigeons out of the coop, chases them off with a long bamboo pole, and then whistles, shouts, claps, waves a flag, or, occasionally, tosses up a firecracker to keep the birds in the air and moving toward a rival ("enemy") stock so that they can mix with it. Then, as the stocks naturally split apart, the flyer calls his birds home. All pigeons, not just the more famous Racing Homers, possess a certain degree of the homing instinct, which can be intensified through breeding and training. As a result, most birds will return to their home loft. However, there are always some birds that become confused and "go lost," as the flyers say of those who fail to return. These are called strays, and they are fair game for any flyer.

The object of the game is to capture these strays from opponents. This is possible because of another instinct the pigeons have, the flock-pull or kit-pull instinct that causes

The beauty of birds in flight. Their aerial maneuvers shift and change, but pigeons tend to remain in a unified pattern, following signals that no scientist has yet been able to decipher.

a lone bird to join any group of pigeons rather than remain isolated in the air. When a flyer spots a stray, he sends up a group of his birds to try to hook it up. When he calls his birds back, the stray will very likely be caught in the pattern of their flight and brought down to their roof. Flyers are, in effect, attempting to overcome their enemies' pigeons will to home. The two instincts are thus at war in the bird, and only a very well-trained pigeon can resist the force of a surrounding flock to break away and return home.

Things may happen quickly or several hours may pass before there is any action. The potential for action exists whenever two or more flyers send their stocks up in the same general area. This happens most often in the afternoon (after working hours) and on weekends, but early morning competition is not unknown. Usually the game is spontaneous and unplanned; flyers do not know who will be sending up birds at any given time, and stocks sent up can vary in size from 30 to 150 birds. Once a flyer's birds have landed, he looks them over for strays and uses a long-handled net called a "hoople" to catch them. By examining a bird he can determine who it belongs to, because all Flights are banded by the time they are two weeks old with both a year band, stating the year of its birth, and a color band that identifies the particular roof to which it belongs. Flyers know who else flies in their neighborhoods and what kind of bands they use.

There are four ways to deal with the birds that are caught, and each flyer makes his own arrangements with his competitors. The first one is "free-catch." This means that the owner of all captured birds is allowed to reclaim them at no cost and is required to give up all birds he catches at no charge. There are also "catches" at a fixed price. This is the same as free-catch except flyers are required to pay a pre-arranged sum, usually about one dollar per bird, to get their pigeons back. This rule makes the game a bit more competitive because money is at stake.

Both systems lend themselves to a practice called "schmocking." Schmocking means a flyer hides and/or refuses to admit he has caught a bird that he is honor-bound to return to its rightful owner. A person schmocks a bird either because it is particularly strong or good-looking and he wants to breed from it, or because he thinks he can sell it for a good price.

Needless to say, schmocking leads to mistrust and bad feeling. It can be avoided by following the third system, "catch-keep." In catch-keep, whatever birds a flyer catches are his to keep; whatever he loses are gone for good. Anyone who agrees with his fellow flyers to follow this system and then tries to bargain for the return of a particular bird ("Just this once!") is known as a

"crybaby" or a "beggar." Many flyers believe that the catch-keep system is what makes the game truly competitive because there is the risk of permanently losing birds. The action is irrevocable.

Most flyers who favor this system do not want their birds back. They believe that if a bird "goes down" where it does not belong, it is not well trained and will never be completely reliable. Since the goal is to develop a tight, dependable stock, they view such losses as part of the natural culling process. "You're better off without it," says Victor Ryder, a fourth-generation pigeon flyer. One year, to test his theory, he bought back sixty of his pigeons that had been caught, and then kept track of them. Fifty-nine "went lost" again.

The final alternative—final in every sense of the word—is "catch-kill," where the pigeon is destroyed. This is used in extreme circumstances, usually in settling personal vendettas or carrying out long-term wars with the bird's owner. There is a saying in the game: "Enemies on the roof, friends in the street." In most instances, as with many competitive sports, this is true. But not always.

To urge his flock up, Victor Ryder uses a homemade "flag"; the vigorous waving motion, along with clapping, shouting, or the occasional tossing of firecrackers, causes the birds to take off and keep moving. When more than one flyer sends up birds, the action begins.

The pigeon game is usually learned through an informal apprenticeship system. Most boys start when they are between six and eleven years of age, rarely after fifteen, and many continue the game for the rest of their lives. Very few women have ever been involved. (There is the legendary "Old Lady Reid" who flew on Reid Avenue in Brooklyn years ago, and I heard rumors of two young girls in Bushwick who sometimes flew with male relatives, but I could not track them down.)

Boys learn from fathers, uncles, older brothers, or neighbors. While being taught how to feed and care for the pigeons and how to develop a good stock of flying birds, they are also being socialized by the values of the game. This is evident, for example, in terms of the attachment a flyer is allowed to feel towards his birds. A young flyer just starting out on his own (who often continues to work as a "chaser," or assistant, for a more established adult) might have only a few birds. Because he has a small stock, it is easier for him to get to know each pigeon individually (not just recognize them). He has closer, more personal contact when he feeds the birds, and he might be keeping them in his house or on his fire escape until he can afford to set up a real coop. If he loses even one, it represents a sizeable percentage of his entire stock. Thus, in the beginning, young flyers often relate to the birds more as pets than as participants in the game. In fact, until their stock gets larger, they cannot really fly the birds competitively. Their attachment to their birds at this stage does not affect the game for anyone else. Young flyers may even have a single favorite bird.

However, as flyers become more involved in the sport and the number of their birds increases, they usually stop having favorite birds. Older flyers are more inclined to feel attached "in general" to the birds as possessions than they are to an individual favorite. In fact, if you ask most adult flyers if they have a favorite bird, they assume you mean a favorite color bird, since it has become so foreign to them to think of having

a single special pigeon. But, if pressed, many of the oldtimers can still recall with fondness one particular pigeon from their childhood.

This change is a natural part of growing up and becoming acculturated within the pigeon world. Affection for an individual bird is acceptable when one is young, has a small stock, and is not truly competitive. But it is scorned among adults, as is any attachment to the birds, whether emotional or economical, that affects a man's willingness to send them up and enter aggressively into the action.

Young flyers are also taught to be responsible. The pigeons are living creatures and must be fed and watered every day. The coops have to be cleaned. During breeding season, flyers must bring up nesting bowls and supplies with which the birds can build their nests. This is a year-round sport, not one that can be left and returned to easily. One young man who found this out for himself was Rapper. He had been a member of a Brooklyn street gang, the Spanish Kings, for three years when a friend invited him to come up to the roof. "I started liking the idea, flying birds. Finally this guy says to me, 'It's either the birds or the gang.' So I picked the birds."

Whitey Betts gives a captured pigeon a careful examination. Because he always plays "catch-keep," Whitey will not return this bird to its original owner. Likewise, when a bird belonging to Whitey is captured, it will not be returned to him.

Whitey Betts, who was partners with Victor Ryder for several years, prepares to capture a stray bird that has come down on his coop. He is using a long-handled net called a "hoople."

Because so many flyers started so early, the game, in a sense, reads like the traditional Bildungsroman: it initiates its hero into adulthood. Over the years, boys become men, and through the game they are offered models that guide them in the acquisition of adult values. The overriding lesson is quite clear: to be good, to be a sport, to be a man, you must always rise to the challenge, take risks, and not be afraid to lose.

When pressed by outsiders for some name by which to identify their sport, flyers generally suggest the "pigeon game," the name I use throughout this article. They rarely use it themselves; they speak only of "action." They say, "How was the action yesterday?" or "I hear there's been a lot of action out by you lately." Erving Goffman has analyzed this term, from its use in the gambler's vocabulary to its use in the streets, and his understanding of it clearly fits the spirit of this sport. Goffman says that action means fateful, eventful activity

entered into for what is believed to be its own sake.[1] A fateful activity is defined as one that is both problematic and consequential—that is, the outcome is uncertain and the player either gains or loses something that is at least subjectively of value to him. One property that distinguishes games and contests from ordinary life is that the time between the initial squaring off, the action itself, and the payoff is relatively short—a more or less discrete activity—whereas in "real" life, the time between choices and actions and consequences may be stretched out over days, months, or years. This makes the game a much more focused activity, a more intense, concentrated experience, and its real importance lies in the fact that this kind of experience offers the participants a chance to test and display their "character," as Goffman sees it: those qualities of courage, gameness or heart, integrity (which is what the schmocker lacks), and composure, qualities

that are not usually called forth by the events of everyday life.[2] Thus, it is not just pigeons that are being risked day after day; it is character that is really on the line.

Risk is central to the game. The whole sport hinges on the players' willingness to engage in these "fateful" moments. This aspect is so important that flyers are divided into two groups, "mutts" and "sports," depending on their attitude toward taking risks. Mutts are cautious and conservative. They keep their pigeons close to home, waiting till a stray comes conveniently close by, until the wind is blowing away from their rivals and toward their own roof before "poking up" any birds. You cannot get much action from a mutt. On the other hand, the highest praise you can give a pi-

geon flyer is to call him a sport. A sport exemplifies the ideal spirit of the game: a willingness to take risks, a joy in playing regardless of the cost. He is not afraid to take chances, because he has discovered the one secret all true gamblers have to learn: To be good, you have to lose.

How much these values affect and carry over into everyday life varies with each individual flyer. The world of the rooftops is very different from the world of the streets, and it would be as naive and simplistic to assume too great a correspondence of values between these two worlds as it would be to assume none at all.

The rooftop location is separate from the everyday world of the streets. Instead of blaring horns and screeching tires, flyers hear the soothing, muted murmur of the birds. Instead of the patterned gridwork of city streets, they have before them vast, un-impeded space, a world without the usual restrictions. Just by being there, the flyer is provided an escape from everyday life that recalls a song by the Drifters from the early sixties:

When this old world starts getting me
    down,
And people are just too much for me to
    face,
I climb way up to the top of the stairs,
And all my cares just drift right into space.

On the roof it's peaceful as can be,
And there the world below can't bother
    me.... [3]

Escape has always been hard to come by in densely populated urban areas, particularly in some of the poor and working class immigrant enclaves where the sport once flourished. People often live closely to-gether, in two- and three-family houses or in tenements packed in tight clusters. Within apartments, space is also scarce, since the majority of flyers have families (or, if they are children, still live with their parents and siblings). Few have the luxury of a private place, let alone a quiet place.[4]

The ethnic backgrounds of many flyers— Italian, Irish, Polish, Jewish, German, and, increasingly, Puerto Rican—often in-clude a strong sense of community. In the Greenpoint-Williamsburg section of Brooklyn, which has one of the heaviest concentrations of flyers, this is most notice-able among the Polish and Italian commu-nities. These groups still have social and political clubs based on ethnicity, still often speak in their mother-tongues, and often frequent certain restaurants and bars that serve as de facto ethnic gathering places. In fact, one effect of the pigeon game (and of the pet shops where the flyers tend to gather) has been to bring together people of different backgrounds who would other-wise have very little contact or interaction.

In these communities of extended fami-lies and social networks, the points at which lives intersect increase the possibili-ties of a person's activities being known by others. People are more visible, and their actions are more public, less anonymous, than they might be in a neighborhood with less ethnic cohesion. Then, too, a lot of ac-tivity takes place in the streets, and word travels fast about who is doing what, with whom, and where. Private troubles have a way of becoming public. For the flyers, the roof provides a real escape from the pres-sures such a community can engender. No one can reach them on the roof. No one can remind them of the money they owe, the job they were supposed to finish, the prob-lems with their wives and families. They are beyond the reach of personal pressures. They may not be able to avoid these prob-lems, but at least for a little while they can literally rise above them. "Up here," says lifelong flyer Whitey Betts, gesturing at his rooftop set-up, "there's no hassles unless you bring them up yourself."

On the roof, flyers are not confronted with barriers of wood or brick or concrete; they are not hemmed in by other buildings, nor do they have buildings looming over them everywhere they turn, making them feel small and somewhat reduced in rela-tion to their environment. Furthermore, their field of operations is no longer broken up into the geometric regularity of city blocks. The space around them is unlim-ited, unbounded, unmarked; there are no corners in the sky.

In these respects, the rooftop can provide refuge for anyone who has access to it; one does not have to be a pigeon flyer to appre-ciate its value as a special place offering peace, quiet, and solitude. However, the flyers have a unique relationship to this space because, for them, the sky is a play-ground. Day after day, the pigeons wheel and dive and roll through it; sometimes they even disappear into it. Then they re-turn. However unconscious, there is a de-gree of identification that takes place in the flyer's mind, just as we all identify with any person or object or activity into which we have invested a great deal of time, effort, and emotional concern. The flight of the birds is significant in terms of the sport because it extends the reach of the flyer—his range of command, his sense of possibility. By itself, the roof already offers an extraordinary sense of open space, a tremendously refreshing change from the congestion of life in the streets. But with the birds, this space is experienced in an even more profound way. It is the last urban wilderness, and the only "range" where a city cowboy has a chance to roam.

The roof also provides the flyer with a "territory." Whether he owns the building or simply rents the space, he usually has control over what goes on there. No one else comes up unless he is invited. The flyer builds the coop or coops where he wants them and in the way he wants them. He may construct a little shanty to protect himself from the elements, and if he does this, the roof can be made habitable: he can bring up a heater, hotplate, radio, portable TV, and lounge chairs. Regardless of the conveniences he does or does not install, the roof still serves as a home away from home. He must go there everyday to feed and water the birds and let them out for exercise, even if he does not have time to engage in any "action." (The birds fly every day, in all weather, unless it is raining heavily or snowing; they slow down during the heat of summer, and autumn tends to be the best season for real competitive flying.) On the roof, a flyer has an authority that stems from his territorial control. He can be neat or messy; eat, sleep, drink, or smoke as he pleases. He directs the activity that goes on. If he feels lazy, he can read the paper and sit in the sun and let the pigeons "bum" all day long. If he feels energetic, he can chase the birds up over and over again. The fact that he is in charge gives the flyer a kind of power that he is hard-pressed to find in his everyday life—a small sphere of influence where he feels free not just because he has escaped *from* something, but because he has assumed sole responsibility *for* and exclusive control *over* something else.

The roofs range from luxurious to decrepit, with most falling somewhere in between. They may be stable and secure, allowing the flyer to establish a lasting domain for himself and his birds. On the other hand, they may have been declared off-limits by an absentee landlord who does not want coops on his roof or they may be extremely vulnerable to theft, in either case, forcing the flyer to relocate frequently and keep his operation fairly portable. Flyers tell about a man in Maspeth, Queens, who they estimate spent between ten and twenty thousand dollars installing indoor-outdoor carpeting in his coops and acquiring the latest security devices. But poor kids just starting out often put their birds on fire escapes or the roofs of abandoned buildings, where they must bring up water by hand every day. On the roofs of certain housing projects where pigeon coops were not allowed, enterprising young flyers managed nonetheless. One of them explained how that worked: "We'd put up a coop on the projects, then the police would come and knock it down. Then we'd put it back up again."

Changes in urban housing and architecture have greatly changed the sport over the last forty years. There used to be hundreds of coops on the tenements of both upper and lower Manhattan, but the advent of huge housing projects virtually eliminated the sport in the Lower East Side and Harlem. Changes in some neighborhoods have brought a whole new generation of pigeon flyers; in Williamsburg and East New York, there are now more black and Hispanic flyers entering what was once primarily the domain of white European immigrants. And although the game still exists (in vastly diminished numbers) in all five boroughs of New York, the highest concentration of flyers is now in Brooklyn, particularly in Canarsie, Bay Ridge, and the Greenpoint-Williamsburg section.

There is another special location associated with the game. This is the pigeon shop, better known as the pet shop, in which flyers can buy everything they need, including the Flights themselves, as well as Racing Homers and nonflying varieties of show pigeons, feed, medicine, and supplies. The pet shop also functions as an informal social club and information center, where flyers come to swap news of wins and losses, give advice, make bets on future action, argue, tease, boast, and generally "break horns" with each other. The shops are especially important to these men because they practice what is often perceived by others to be a "deviant" and "anti-social" activity; the pet shop offers a context in which the flyers can see themselves as normal and acceptable—even respected and admired—members of a group.

I discovered the sport in 1978 in the Greenspoint-Williamsburg section of Brooklyn and was hooked right away. I spent weeks on the rooftops and in the pigeon stores, observing the game and getting to know the flyers. But every time I asked someone directly what it was about the game that appealed to him, he would just shrug and say, "It's a hobby." I asked one sixteen-year-old boy if he ever talked about the birds to his classmates. He shook his head and answered, "No, they don't know what it is to have pigeons. They wouldn't understand." A much older flyer interrupted. "You don't really talk to people that don't know about it," he said. "They think you belong in an insane asylum."

The pet shop further serves as a kind of figurative archive of pigeon lore. This is where stories and legends are exchanged and elaborated on, then stored in the memories of the flyers, to be taken out of their

Freddie Manzi, Whitey Betts, and Victor Ryder examine a bird in a pigeon shop, where it is possible to buy birds, feed, and medicine. Many flyers gather in these shops, which have become clubhouses and social centers for the sport.

A stock of pigeons descends to its home roof as darkness falls. Pigeons are brought in at night, and corn is sometimes tossed out to lure in any birds that are reluctant to stop flying.

mental files and recounted to other members of their select community on appropriate occasions (such as any Friday night when flyers have gathered to drink coffee or beer around the table in the pet shop).

When I first met the pigeon flyers, their sport was already dying out. A few pockets of intense activity still survived in Brooklyn, and there was sporadic action elsewhere. Flyers estimated at that time that there were perhaps five hundred active roofs citywide. The end of the road was in sight, they said, and in another twenty-five to fifty years this variation of the sport would probably be completely gone. Unfortunately, the end seems even closer than that, due to a rather cruel blow from nature. In 1985, the New York area's domesticated pigeon population was struck with Newcastle's disease, a poultry virus that had earlier invaded some Maryland and Pennsylvania chicken farms. Never in anyone's memory had such a disease swept so rapidly and so fatally through the rooftops. Stock after stock was destroyed, thousands of birds, and when it finally seemed under control (after a massive vaccination program), many flyers had lost everything. Quite a few of the oldtimers called it quits, too disheartened to begin again.

But not all of them. You can still look up—especially on clear, crisp autumn days—and see flocks of pigeons swoop and dive in dazzling aerial maneuvers, their white wingtips sparkling in the sunlight like tiny mirrors flashing codes across the sky. For now, anyway, the skies over Brooklyn are still alive.

NOTES

1. Erving Goffman, "Where the Action Is," *Interaction Ritual: Essays on Face-to-Face Behavior* (Garden City, New York: Anchor Books/ Doubleday and Co., 1967), 185.
2. *Ibid.*, 218–19.
3. "Up On the Roof," by Gerry Goffin and Carole King (Screen Gems-Columbia, BMI, 1961).

4. One of the best descriptions of the everyday noise of tenement life can be found in Daniel Fuchs's Williamsburg trilogy—almost every novelist who has chronicled immigrant life in New York has dealt with this problem. Daniel Fuchs, *Three Novels: Summer in Williamsburg, Homage to Blenholt, Low Country* (New York: Basic Books, 1961).

Debatable Land

Frontier Versus Wilderness in the Ozark National Scenic Riverways

BY ERIKA BRADY

A community defines its identity as much by the beliefs and behavior it rejects as by those it values. Its members contrast their own "proper" behavior with the unacceptable manners and mannerisms of nonmembers in order to validate their own view of themselves and the world.[1] This process of definition by contrast takes place even among groups that have lived side by side for generations.

The introduction of the automobile to the general public in the early part of this century added a new dimension to this habit of mind, for a dramatic increase in tourism brought unprecedented numbers of strangers to regions hitherto isolated. These newcomers were often drawn by exotic hearsay concerning the "natives," and the inhabitants of the region have often been primed for the visitors by equally exotic tales of wickedness and excess that characterize regions outside their own.

When visitor and inhabitant meet and these myths converge in a single location, the results range from diverting to tragic. Unless some mediation or interpretation occurs, both parties usually return home with their preconceptions confirmed. But

Canoeists on the Jacks Fork and Current rivers. The rivers have been used for leisurely "floats" for most of the century, but today, as great numbers of people invade the area each summer, the experience has become significantly different than it was in the early years. Courtesy of the National Park Service, Ozark National Scenic Riverways

when the number of visitors grows to the point that the resources of the region for both tourism and other local interests become overextended and regulations are imposed by outside institutions, the negative stereotypes on both sides are not only reinforced but intensified. The divergence between the two worlds, their view of one another and their view of the territory under dispute, becomes unbridgeable and potentially violent.

My own research in such an area began in 1986 with a conflict over the legality of furtrapping in the portions of the Jacks Fork and Current rivers in Missouri administered by the National Park Service as the Ozark National Scenic Riverways, established by Congress in 1964 as the first of a series of "national riverways."[2] Independent of the Park Service, I undertook a study of trapping as a traditional activity in the region. Interviewing trappers, I soon discovered the necessity of budgeting my time and recording tape to accommodate an initial ten minutes or so of angry discussion concerning the suit brought by the Missouri Trappers Association against the National Park Service, and problems in the Riverways in general. While trappers and many others interviewed in the region expressed strong feelings concerning the specific events related to the brief ban on trapping (and numerous other more or less predictable grievances against the Park Service), it became apparent to me that the greater part of local anger was directed elsewhere—toward the recent invasion in unprecedented numbers of "floaters" on the streams.

Local people were bitter about recurrent objectionable behavior of visitors and resentful about the contempt they felt directed at themselves as "hillbilly savages." They were especially enraged that policy within the Riverways was determined by outsiders and apparently from a view of nature and land use both foreign and repugnant to the inhabitants. The Ozarkers who fish, hunt, trap, and picnic along these rivers travel symbolic waters that are very different from those enjoyed by most outsiders, who pour in on weekends and summer holidays. The history of these di-

MISSOURI

MISSOURI'S 7 VACATIONLANDS

(Key list and small map refer to yellow out-lined areas on large map)

1. PONY EXPRESS REGION
2. MARK TWAIN REGION
3. KANSAS CITY AREA
4. LAKE OF THE OZARKS REGION
5. ST. LOUIS AREA
6. OZARK PLAYGROUND REGION
7. BIG SPRINGS REGION

A tourist map from the Missouri Division of Tourism, 1977, shows the state's many recreational areas. The Jacks Fork and Current rivers are in section 7. Geography and Map Division, Library of Congress

vergent points of view is worth examining, for it reveals much about the character of the state and region, and the nature of such conflicts wherever they occur.

Missouri as a whole presents a problem for those who prefer clear regional and cultural boundaries. Comprising the north-

ern perimeter of the South and the southern perimeter of the Midwest, Missouri also represents the "gateway to the West," a historical role symbolized by the splendid Gateway Arch of St. Louis and still enacted in the rivalry between that city's temperate gentility and the brasher prairie temper of Kansas City. Even the pronunciation of the state's name is a matter of dispute: some say *Mizzuree*, some *Mizzurah*, and a diehard handful insist that the only literate usage calls for a "miss," not a "miz," in the first syllable. The entire state is a bastion of ambiguity.

Roughly half the state lies in the geographical and cultural region called the Ozarks. As a result of Al Capp's cartoons, tireless commercial promotion, and a quantity of sentimental fiction published in the early twentieth century, those who have never visited the Ozarks think they know what to expect there: lawless illiterates, skinny dogs, and ballad-warbling granny women, all of whom may be bypassed by the visitor seeking escape from civilization in the unspoiled rivers and virgin forests. It is an outsider's image projected on many regions throughout the hills and mountains of the South.

In reality, the Ozarks confounds simple images. The very name represents a linguistic peculiarity: from an abbreviation of the French *aux Arcansas* ("to Arkansas"), it must be one of the few American placenames derived from a prepositional phrase. Although most of the terrain is hill country, it varies from the regular roll of the verdant prairies near the Mississippi to the rough slopes and knobby outcroppings of the central region. Most of the inhabitants are of Scots-Irish stock, but one can still speak French with descendants of eighteenth-century miners in Washington County, or German with descendants of nineteenth-century Missouri Synod Lutherans in towns with names such as Altenberg and Wittenberg.

Despite these anomalies, it is possible to observe certain generalities. Cultural geographer Milton D. Rafferty has described several distinctive traits of Ozark life. It is primarily rural, drawing on a heritage rooted in the southern Uplands. The social system is relatively stable, despite many areas currently enduring severe economic stress. Children grow up within extended families that have often worked the same woods, fields, and rivers for generations.

Perhaps as a result of this stability, Ozarkers display a powerful sense of place. Unlike the term *Appalachia* in the eastern South, a term fostered as a result of poverty programs in the sixties, *Ozark* is a term of

pride in the region and is used frequently in the naming of businesses and organizations, especially in southwest Missouri. In addition to this general regional identification, the Ozarker seemingly relishes a kind of localized "claiming by naming": the density of formal and informal placenames for physical features and communities is formidable, and their poetic ingenuity is dazzling.[3] Virtually every quarter of a mile on Jacks Fork and Current rivers, for example, is designated by a descriptive name recalling a notable feature, a favored use, or an animal or human denizen.

Not only are the placenaming practices of Ozarkers proprietary, their own identification with others as part of their communal landscape is highly exclusive. An Ozark address does not constitute membership as an insider in the community or region, even when maintained over decades. The conservatism of the region is well expressed by historian Robert Flanders's characterization of the region as a "perpetuated frontier." Traditional lifestyles are vigorously maintained in conscious contrast to "outsider" behavior, sometimes at the expense of technological and economic improvement.[4]

The term *frontier* in Ozark usage invokes the historic era of settlement in the eighteenth and early nineteenth centuries, from which many inhabitants can trace direct descent. To the Ozarker, the term also invokes the varied repertoire of skills and crafts initially related to subsistence during the earliest period in this demanding country, including hunting, trapping, fishing, beekeeping, and rootdigging. Although most Ozark families no longer depend outright on these activities for subsistence, they are still enthusiastically pursued.

Using one's skills to add a bit to the family bank account or put a savory oldtime meal on the dinner table represents a form of "productive recreation" much valued by Ozarkers, who regard such pursuits both pragmatically, as secondary economic assets in an area where many list their calling as "jack-of-all-trades," and sentimentally, as links with a proud and colorful past when such skills were indispensable. Like their British forebears, they view prece-

dence as ultimate vindication of their rights with regard to such activities. When long-standing practices that combine subsistence and sentiment come into conflict with authority or opinion imposed by outsiders, Ozarkers can be extraordinarily unyielding, whether the issue is bearing firearms, manufacturing moonshine, or maintaining pasturage by burning.

Valuable furs from the rivers and forests and minerals from the hills first brought Europeans to the Ozarks in the late seventeenth century. The French priest Father Membre remarked of the region in 1688 that "Our hunters, French and Indian, are delighted with the country."[5] The swift-running rivers transversing the hills country not only provided habitat for mink, muskrat, beaver, bobcat, bear, deer, otter, and raccoon, but also offered a means of transporting the pelts to the trading posts located along the Mississippi River to the east. The timber boom of the late nineteenth and early twentieth centuries shifted the means of commercial transport from

the rivers and poor roads to the railways newly built by the industry. Although the primary transportation of timber from the region was by rail, location of timber manufacturing centers near rivers was practical because the streams were useful for short-haul transport of logs. The most aggressive lumbering took place in the region of the Current River and Jacks Fork, wiping out the virgin stands of shortleaf pine.

Despite the devastating effects of deforestation in this area of the Ozarks, the gradual withdrawal of the timber companies in the first decades of the twentieth century brought tourism in its wake as a new and unexpected industry. The float fishing excursion of Missouri Governor Herbert S. Hadley in 1909 represented a landmark in local history. Governor Hadley and more than forty businessmen, officials, guides, and newsmen boarded flat-bottomed boats

Above: Workers on the Current River direct newly cut timber downstream to railheads, about 1910. No longer on the river, the timber industry is still an economic force in the region. Courtesy of the National Park Service, Ozark National Scenic Riverways

Right: In this 1906 stereopticon view, an Ozark guide calls his camper's attention to a point of interest on the Current River. Courtesy of the National Park Service, Ozark National Scenic Riverways

at Welch Cave, arriving downstream at Round Spring the next day. Thanks to careful planning by the organizers, the trip received national attention, and the Ozarks began to command interest as a sportsman's haven.[6] The rivers had always represented an aesthetic as well as practical boon to those living nearby—since Governor Hadley's time, the reduction of timbering and decline in mining in the area has transformed that beauty into the area's most valuable commercial resource.

By the late 1950s, second growth of oak and hickory had replaced the pine forests lost to the timber boom along much of the river banks, and float trips for those hardy and skillful enough to pursue them were experiences to describe in rapturous superlatives. Floating the rivers not only offered fine fishing and incomparable scenery but also the opportunity to discover the culture of the region through the agency of local guides, who often assisted the same floaters year after year. At the time, the villain in the romance seemed the ubiquitous Army Corps of Engineers, which periodically threatened to end this idyll by damming the Current River. Although the efforts of the Corps were unsuccessful, the mere attempts horrified writer Leonard Hall, an ardent lover of the Current and Jacks Fork. Partly in response to this menace, he wrote *Stars Upstream: Life Along an Ozark River.* Published in 1958, this classic of the American outdoors introduced the charms of the area to a wide audience and played a critical role in bringing about the legislation establishing the Riverways under federal control under the administration of the National Park Service rather than the Army Corps of Engineers.[7]

Hall's book remains a delight to read, despite the fact that "life along the Ozark rivers" in question has changed irrevocably, in part as a result of his eloquence. Hall drastically underestimated the allure of his rivers, once discovered: he predicted that recreational use of the Current and its tributaries would always be effectively limited by the character of the rivers, enumerating their chill and swiftness, the annoyance of biting insects, and the skill required to canoe and camp as factors that would protect the streams from overuse.

Hall and others who fostered the idea of the Riverways envisioned a wilderness protected, in which activities such as hunting, trapping, and fishing would continue as before, while forms of exploitation destructive to the habitat would be prevented. New users drawn to the region would be a special, elite breed—responsible and sensitive to ecological issues. Hall knew well that the rivers had endured perilous cycles of commercialization and were, in environmental terms, far from virginal. But he recognized a symbolic purity in the beauty renewed out

of previous depredations. Not in the least naive concerning the rivers' commercial past, he was extraordinarily naive concerning the rivers' recreational future.

Unfortunately, despite cold water and nasty mosquitoes, the Jacks Fork and Current rivers are visited by hordes so eager for a taste of wilderness they are willing to share the feast with any number of others at the same time. In 1972, the first year statistics were kept, Park Service officials estimate that the 130-mile length of the Riverways carried approximately 120,000 canoeists and 14,000 powerboaters. In 1979, the first year in which tubers were systematically included in user counts, they numbered more than 15,000. In 1987, estimates were up to 190,000 canoeists, 35,000 powerboaters, and 35,000 tube-floaters—the latter apparently quite happy to float downstream in the chilly water that Leonard Hall hoped would discourage casual users.

The Riverways has never provided the economic boost to the region that inhabitants and local politicians had hoped. The region remains among the poorest in Missouri: in 1986, the six counties affected included the counties rated first and second in unemployment in the state. That same year, the mean salary of the six counties averaged $6,293.[8] Those owning the regulated canoe concessions have profited, but the general impression among locals is that the economic benefits have been disappointing.

Friendly contact with outsiders has actually diminished. No longer do most visitors float decorously downstream under the guidance of a familiar Ozarker. Canoes or tubes are rented from the concessions, and both the personal and economic interaction between visitors and inhabitants is often limited to the exchange of a few bills at that time: locals claim that the typical floater arrives with a ten-dollar bill and a pair of cut-off jeans—and when he leaves a few days later he hasn't changed either one.

Assuming, locals might add, that he's still wearing his pants. There are many reasons

why visitors are drawn to the Riverways: some seek a social experience in a scenic setting, some seek a natural experience in a controlled setting. But there is no question which visitors are the source of greatest concern to local people: the uninhibited ones who engage in hijinks involving nudity, sexual misconduct, and drug use scandalize local observers every summer. Negative feelings concerning outsider use of the Riverways crystallize in discussions of such behavior, which becomes generalized to characterize all visitors.

While some city dwellers perceive the rivers as wild, untamed, and innocent arenas for their own wild, untamed, and far-from-innocent horseplay, inhabitants of the region see a familiar part of their "back yard" and a valued productive resource now fouled by visitors' language, sexual exhibitionism, drunkenness, and other offensive behavior. Many who claim proudly that they were "raised on the river" now refuse to go there at all, or limit their visits to winter months when the "outsider" traffic is light. For their part, visitors often seem to regard the local people as threatening intruders in a riverbank Eden, invaders from *Deliverance*-land given to irrational and unprovoked fits of temper. Both sides admit exceptions to the rule—the helpful and humorous local, the decent and sportsmanlike canoeist. But overcrowding on the river has tended to reinforce stereotypes and polarize relations.

A perfect example of divergence in attitudes may be seen in local peoples' response to nudity on the river. Naked swimming, regarded by some visitors as an appropriate expression of escape from the trammels of civilization, is regarded as seriously offensive by local people, especially if it occurs in mixed groups, or if a naked man makes no effort to hide himself before women and children who may unexpectedly come on the scene. Vance Randolph remarked on the habitual sexual prudery of Ozark vocabulary in mixed company in his day, and although verbal taboos have somewhat loosened, those concerning actions perceived as sexually provocative or aggressive remain strong.[9] A Salem woman recounted a typical episode:

In the summer, this guy walked right by us, had his Levis on, his cut-offs in his hand, walked right by us, went down past, right in front of us, didn't try and hide or anything, took off his jeans, RIGHT down to the bare . . . skin, didn't *turn* his back to *us*, he turned his back to the *river* and faced *us!* That's like they do in Florida, and all these other places like that! You've heard of it for a long time, but this is just as bad or worse.[10]

A whole cycle of stories told throughout the area recount the revenge, violent or prankish, wrought on the outsider foolish enough to expose himself without shame to the wife and family of an Ozark man:

I can't think of this fella's name, but he's a great big fella, and was raised on the river, and of course he had his family on the river, and these people came down, and they were going to take their clothes off—*did* take their clothes off right around his wife and children. And just right out in the open, didn't hide theirself or anything. So he told his wife and his two children to get in the pickup and go up the road. And he thought all the time, "Now, I'm gonna have to do *something*. I don't know what I'm going to do." There were men and women both, and he didn't know what to do.
So he made up his mind what he thought he might do. He got his wife and children and they got in the pickup and left. And he got up in the bush. He always wore big overalls and a pair of big ol' brogan shoes. So he took his overalls off, and stripped down to his birthday suit—and this guy weighs about 250 pounds—woolly-looking fella. He left his brogan shoes on so he wouldn't hurt his feet on the rocks. And he come crashing out of the rocks, and he come crashing out of the brush, and he says, "I WANT TO MAKE A BABY! I WANT TO MAKE A BABY!" And he said they went to go in the canoes like fowl. He broke up their nude party pretty rapidly!

Sometimes an account of a face-off involves a more serious threat, albeit with comical overtones:

There was a man and his wife in a jon boat, and of course they had a .22 rifle. And of course they had this for—everyone carries a gun down here. Almost everyone. And we don't carry it for any violent reason, but we just always carry a gun, and

that's just part of our dress. Anyway, he had his .22 in the boat, and he and his wife were fishing. And they got down the river, and there was a big deep hole of water down there with a tree growed out over it, and this fella was high on drugs, or drunk, or something, and he was setting up, up in this tree without any clothes on, and he told this fella, he said, "I'm gonna jump out on your wife, when you float under the tree." And this fella said, "Naw, I'll save you the trouble, I'll just shoot ya out." And he grabbed the .22, and about the time he grabbed the .22, the fella slid out of the tree backwards so fast he's like to have killed hisself.

Many local people are not only offended by the uninhibited behavior of floaters, but actively fear them, as this conversation among several trappers and their wives reveals:

HG: Carrie Lee thinks it's dangerous, don't you, Carrie Lee?
MA: I think so too!
Interviewer: How do you mean, dangerous? The people . . .
MA: The tourists, yeah. They're on dope—Yeah, there's a lot of drinking, but there's more narcotics—
CLA: More narcotics, bad language—
MA: Awful language, it's terrible.
HG: It's terrible.
MA: Well, one lady was camped there on a campsite right next to the river, and these canoeists came down through there, and she has a daughter that's about ten, I guess, and this man and lady got out of the canoe and had sex *right there* and then they propositioned that little ten-year-old girl to have it with them too. Now what do you expect out of something like *that*, now? They don't want trapping—do away with "harming the animals"—but you can harm these human beings all you want to, it's fine.
You oughta be down there sometimes. I tell you, I watch what my kid watches on TV and I banned a lot of these TV shows. But you go to the river and you've got triple-X-rated movies all day long.

Even when the visitors are not present, they leave offensive reminders of their presence. A group of local people recalled a fishing expedition they made to the very point at which Governor Hadley embarked on his epoch-making float trip in 1909:

OP: You know two or three years ago, when you went with me down to Welch's Cave?

JA: Couldn't stand it.

HP: [wife]: Ooh, I remember what I was saying, "Though I walk through this Valley of Death, I fear no evil . . ." [laughs] and them just laughed at me.

OP: We couldn't even park, we had to pull back up on the road, and I wanted to go fishing. It's not quite a quarter mile up there to the spring, is it, and there's a trail that used to go up there to this Welch's Cave Spring. And I was gonna go up there and fish. And there's come a little shower of rain right after noon that day [laughter], and then the sun came out, and the moisture and humidity was high in there, and it was so bad—

JA: Worst bathroom you were ever into.

OP: The people in canoes'd just go out down that trail, you know [sighs].

When I first began work on this project, well-meaning friends in the small city on the fringe of the Ozarks where I live warned me repeatedly about the dangers of dealing with the men and women of the area. Violence, incest, perversion, and general lawlessness were what I could expect to find. "Just like *Deliverance*," my supporters would nod knowingly, basing their knowledge on hearsay, crime reports in the *St. Louis Post-Dispatch,* and a sensational 1972 movie based on James Dickey's fictional account of a canoe trip in north Georgia. While no inhabitants of the Current River area would deny that the region is socially and economically troubled in many respects, they see the *Deliverance* label frequently leveled at them from a different point of view:

AG: To me, *Deliverance*—you just turn everything right reverse to that *Deliverance* deal, only you got more people here—you see more in a day's time than *Deliverance* even thought about!

HG: It's not from the local people. It's from the people that are away from here that is more like in *Deliverance*. In *Deliverance,* it was the local people getting even with the floaters, but here it's right reverse, it's the out-of-town people that've been really cruel to the local people.

AG: Oh, we're mean and bad, because we run 'em off round here because they run around nude having sex right in front of the family. We're cruel!

HG: It don't make sense.

It would be easy to dismiss the Ozarkers' cycles of stories and complaints concerning outsiders on the river as the individual grumblings of bitter, jealous men and women who would prefer a return to a simpler era when the natural resources of the region were their own domain, to be gathered, shared, or hoarded at will. Examination of their stories and grievances, however, reveals a defensible rationale for their concern—a rationale consistent with their traditional and ongoing relationship with the land, and compatible with the legal mandate of the Ozark National Scenic Riverways.

To the Ozarkers of the region, the rivers are a part of a social as well as a geographic landscape. Despite the privacy one may enjoy there, they are public not only in the legal sense presently applicable but also public in the older sense of being "of and for members of the community." Most adults remember not only the time prior to the establishment of the Riverways when ownership of the land along the rivers was

In mid-December, trapper Kenneth Wells has a stretch of the Upper Current River to himself. Photograph by Erika Brady, 1986

in private hands but also exactly who owned specific stretches in their area. Men and women know the names and local associations for every stretch of the river in their region in exactly the sense that city dwellers can recite every shop and family home on the block where they grew up.

River territory for Ozarkers, therefore, remains space in which one is socially accountable. Historically the commercial highway of the region, the river is also a social space comparable to the "front lawn" of urban dwellers—private or socially unacceptable behavior is better performed away from the riverbanks and paths, where accidental interruptions are less likely to occur.

For those outsiders whose behavior so offends local people, on the other hand, the river delights precisely because it is territory within which they are unaccountable for their behavior, far from the control of their own social milieu. They can and do revert with impunity to adolescent, even infantile behavior. Their own presence and that of other human beings on the river they regard as incidental. Nothing is required of them in the face of the immensity of nature's apparent preeminence; they have no weight in nature's balance. Their image of the Riverways as "perpetuated wilderness" implies a limitless power of the stream to absolve them of responsibility for their behavior and absorb their waste without consequence.

Just as locals tend to generalize the worst visitor behavior in characterizing all visitors, Ozark trappers are, to many outsiders, a lawless and wantonly cruel pack of mavericks representing city dwellers' most frightening woodland fantasies. In fact, trappers of the region represent one of the most stable and controlled groups with an economic interest in the river. Under careful seasonal regulation by the state, the same men tend to divide up the portions of the river in their areas, trap the same stretches year after year, and monitor one another's practices. Thanks to the efforts of the Mis-

souri Department of Conservation since the 1930s and the cooperation of local trappers, populations of local furbearering animals have never been stronger. Some species virtually trapped out in the early part of the century are now back in such numbers that they represent a problem. As a result, the dwellers in this "perpetuated frontier" have adopted a new design for their relationship with the local ecology in which the old image of "consumption of unlimited resources" has been replaced by procedures drawn from an agrarian model.

Seeing themselves directly involved in the ecological systems of the region, many trappers regard themselves as responsible for the welfare of the species. They strive to reduce populations just enough to ensure an adequate supply of food for the remainder. In the trappers' view, their presence in the ecosystem of the region is neither incidental nor accidental, and they regard any image of the Riverways as a perpetuated wilderness in the strict sense as both misguided and historically inaccurate:

We've put our thumb on the scale of nature. And you can't just take it off and say things are gonna be like they were. Because they'll never *be* like they were—we haven't got the habitat. They call the Ozark National Scenic Riverways the way it was a hundred years ago—it's *not*. It's not and never will be again.

To one extent or another, this attitude toward the Riverways is typical of the region. A "frontier" domain, after all, implies an active engagement with the region: a grappling with the terms the land lays down for survival.

There are no easy answers to the issues raised by conflicting images of frontier and wilderness in the Ozark National Scenic Riverways—no simple criterion defining the rights of any single group. The local canons of precedent, sentiment, and survival have no legal weight, yet must be taken into account if equitable decisions of policy are to be made. In microcosm, the problems of this region represent similar difficulties being addressed with varying consequences throughout the National Park Service, and indeed, anywhere that is "discovered" by tourists eager to escape temporarily from the pressures and demands of their own worlds.

While the National Park Service copes with the ecological results of the unexpected popularity of the Riverways, the human drama continues with little successful mediation. Where once there existed the opportunity, however tenuous, for mutual learning and exchange between people living very different lives, fewer and fewer such opportunities are offered or sought. Trapper Kenneth Wells told me a quiet little story that sums up the finality of the division. While on his way to fish at Parker Ford, he saw a woman sunbathing nude on a gravelbank near his path. Embarrassed, he hovered at a distance for a bit.

Well, she finally saw me, and I was probably thirty yards [away] when she saw me. So she politely walked into the tent. Now her husband was setting outside the tent. She didn't get into any hurry! But I just went on down there and went fishing. And went away on down the river, and when I came back, she was dressed. And you know what she made the comment? She says, "Is this the river they trap on?" I says, "Yes, ma'am." [She says] "Boy, they oughtn't to be allowed to trap." I never said a word, Erika, I just kept walking.

NOTES

I am grateful to the Eastern National Park and Monument Association, which awarded me a Herbert E. Kahler Research Fellowship to pursue my investigation of the Ozark Riverways. Thanks also are due to Congressman Bill Emerson, of Missouri's Eighth District, and his staff in Washington and Cape Girardeau; and to Arthur Sullivan, superintendent of the Ozark National Scenic Riverways, National Park Service, Van Buren, Missouri, and staff members Jim Corless, Alex Outlaw, and Jim Simpson. Above all, my gratitude goes to the members of the ninth district of the Missouri Trappers Association, under the leadership of Kenneth Wells, whose cooperation made this study possible.

1. This factor has long been recognized by folklorists, many of whom have adopted the concept of an "esoteric-exoteric factor" elucidated by the work of William Hugh Jansen. See, for example, William Hugh Jansen, "The Esoteric-Exoteric Factor in Folklore," *Fabula: Journal of Folktale Studies* 2 (1959): 205–11.

2. Public Law 88-492, which established the Ozark National Scenic Riverways, included specific provisions permitting hunting and fishing in the region. Trapping was considered to be a form of hunting and continued uninterrupted in the Riverways from its inception. In 1984, however, the Department of the Interior moved to ban all activities not specifically mentioned as permissible by the enabling legislation of a park. The ban was to take effect in the Riverways beginning with the trapping season of winter 1986–87.

After considerable legislative and judicial wrangling, the Missouri Trappers Association brought suit against the National Park Service. In 1988, the case was resolved in favor of the Trappers Association, and the Park Service was enjoined from enforcing the ban.

3. Milton D. Rafferty, *The Ozarks: Land and Life* (Norman: University of Oklahoma Press, 1980), 4–6.

4. Theodore Russell Pease, *A Connecticut Yankee in the Frontier Ozarks: The Writings of Theodore Pease Russell,* ed. James F. Keefe and Lynn Morrow, with an introduction by Robert Flanders (Columbia: University of Missouri Press, 1988), iv. The concepts of "frontier" and "wilderness" in broader historical terms were explored by Roderick Nash, *Wilderness and the American Mind* (New Haven: Yale University Press, 1967).

5. Quoted in Louis Houck, *A History of Missouri,* vol. 1 (Chicago: R. R. Donnelley and Sons, 1908), 34.

6. Rafferty, 200–202.

7. Leonard Hall, *Stars Upstream: Life Along an Ozark River* (Chicago: University of Chicago Press, 1958). Reference to the importance of this book in the establishment of the ONSR may be found in the foreword of the 1969 edition (University of Missouri Press) written by George P. Hartzog, Jr., then director of the National Park Service.

8. Arthur L. Sullivan, superintendent, Ozark National Scenic Riverways, "A Report on Trapping Within the Ozark National Scenic Riverways," in response to a request from Congressman Bruce F. Vento, Subcommittee on National Parks and Recreation, and Congressman Bill Emerson, Eighth District, Missouri. Report dated May 1, 1986.

9. Vance Randolph, "Verbal Modesty in the Ozarks," *Dialect Notes* 5 (1929), reprinted in *Ozark, Ozark: A Hillside Reader,* ed. Miller Williams (Columbia: University of Missouri Press, 1981), 33–40.

10. Stories and conversations are transcribed from tape-recorded interviews made in the course of the trapping investigation. Copies of these tapes will be deposited at the Western Historical Manuscripts Division of the University of Missouri-Columbia and the American Folklife Center's Archive of Folk Culture at the Library of Congress on completion of the project. Access will be restricted until 1995.

Finding the "True America"

Ethnic Tourism in New Mexico During the New Deal

BY MARTA WEIGLE

Colorful New Mexico will be more colorful than ever [in 1940]. To the regular summer events and celebrations that attract visitors from throughout the world [will] be [added] the [Coronado] Entradas and the nearly two hundred folk festivals scattered throughout the state all during the summer.
—*Edmund Sherman,*
"New Mexico Celebrates,"
New Mexico Magazine, *June 1940*

By 1940 northern New Mexico and northern Arizona were firmly established centers of tourism in the United States. After 1901, the Atchison, Topeka & Santa Fe Railway and, in close association, the Fred Harvey Company had promoted the Grand Canyon as a premier attraction for what Nelson H. H. Graburn calls Nature tourism, "where varied aspects of the land, sea, and sky perform their magical works of renewal." The popular Grand Canyon complex of accommodations, lookout spots, and guided trips also fostered what Graburn identifies as Ethnic tourism, claiming that, for some tourists,

Nature in the "raw" is nice but somewhat boring because there is no dialogue. . . .

Another way to get close to Nature's bosom is through her children, the people of Nature, once labeled Peasant and Primitive peoples and considered creatures of instinct. Interaction with them is possible and their naturalness and simplicity exemplifies all that is good in Nature herself.[1]

At the Grand Canyon, the principal ethnic peoples on display and available for "interaction" were Hopis and Navajos, especially in the Mary Colter-designed Hopi House (opened 1905) and Hopi Watchtower (opened 1932).

Ethnic tourism facilities at the Grand Canyon were patterned after the Fred Harvey Indian Building (with interiors by Mary Colter), opened on the station platform at Albuquerque in 1902. Santa Fe passengers were funneled between "live" Indians on the platform into the building's museum room, which displayed fine examples of Native American and Hispanic arts. From there they moved through a demonstration room with "real" Indian artists at work and a retail room with "authentic" items for sale, before being sent to accommodations in the next-door Alvarado Hotel. The famous Alvarado (opened 1902, demolished 1970) was built in California Spanish-Mission style, but Hispanic folk arts and culture were not securely harnessed to the Harvey-Santa Fe system until the railroad bought La Fonda on the Santa Fe Plaza. By 1929 this "Inn at the End of the Trail" had been redesigned for the Fred Harvey Company in Spanish-Pueblo style by architect John Gaw Meem and featured predominantly Mexican/Spanish colonial interiors by Mary Colter.

La Fonda served as the headquarters for the Fred Harvey Indian Detours. Launched in 1926, the company offered chauffeured and guided car tours away from the tracks and stationside facilities into Pueblo and Hispanic communities in the northern Rio Grande Valley, throughout Navajo and Hopi country, and to natural wonders not served by the railroads, such as Mesa Verde and Carlsbad Caverns. In an August 1925 promotional talk in Santa Fe, Detours founder R. Hunter Clarkson asserted: "There is more of historic, prehistoric, human and scenic interest in New Mexico

"Acoma Pueblo woman wearing typical dress and silver and turquoise bracelets and beads of Indian craftsmanship." This is one of a number of photographs by Laura Gilpin contributed for use in New Mexico: A Guide to the Colorful State. *(LC-USZ62-36220) Prints and Photographs Division, Library of Congress*

Meeting the train to sell pottery, Pueblo of La-guana, New Mexico, 1902. (LC-USZ62-047842) De-troit Publishing Co., Prints and Photographs Division, Library of Congress

than in any other similar area of the world, not excepting India, Egypt, Europe or Asia," and claimed that "the big idea [of Indian Detours] is not only to let people know what is in Northern New Mexico but to tell them what it is when they see it." Thunderbird-emblazoned Harveycars were driven by chauffeur-mechanics dressed as cowboys. Trained guides known as Couriers accompanied each group of Harveycar Indian Detourists. Couriers were young Anglo women uniformed like Navajo "maidens." According to an Indian Detours brochure of 1933:

Couriers' attractive outing uniforms, rich in Navajo hammered silver and turquoise jewelry, are characteristic of the Southwestern Indian country. Greeting guests on arrival by train, it is thereafter the Couriers' privilege to fill the pleasant dual role of hostesses as well as guides. . . . Friendships with representative Indians in many pueblos assure their guests intimate glimpses of Indian life not otherwise obtainable.

The economic and symbolic control exercised by railroads, chauffeured vehicles, and professional interpreters mediating aesthetic tastes and interpersonal encounters weakened as growing numbers of automobiles and improved roads freed tourists from timetables, tracks, and tour guides. In 1930 the New Mexico Highway Department started a Service Bureau to answer travelers' inquiries and, in June 1933, organized a highway patrol to assure safety on the roads and to offer visitors information, welcome, and goodwill. Relief workers on the New Deal's Public Works Project began roadside beautification in March 1934 and erected signs and markers for tourists. An advertising program was launched in 1934 with help from an association of state businessmen known as the Tourist Development League. In 1935 newly inaugurated Governor Clyde Tingley reorganized the Highway Department and created the New Mexico Tourist Bureau to coordinate all state and civic activities aimed at developing tourism. Tourism also received a boost from the American Guide project of the Works Progress Administration's Federal Writers' Project (FWP), begun nationally on August 2, 1935, and in New Mexico on October 15 of that year.

The Sante Fe Railroad depot (far left), the Indian Building (to the right of it), and the Alvarado Hotel, Albuquerque, New Mexico, 1903. The juxtaposition of the three structures symbolizes the linkage of the railroad, the tourist trade, and the sale of Indian and Hispanic crafts from the region. (LC-USZ62-46258) Detroit Photographic Co., Prints and Photographs Division, Library of Congress

The American Guide Series was initially conceived as a five-volume, regional (Northeast, Southeast, North Central, South Central, and Pacific Coast) encyclopedia written in Washington, D.C., from information supplied by state writers on work relief. However, by October 1935, the national office modified this proposal to concentrate on state guides locally written and edited on both state and national levels. Federal Writers' Project director Henry G. Alsberg, associate FWP director George Cronyn, and Katherine Kellock, who became the national office's tour director, disagreed about the guidebooks' character.

Alsberg and Cronyn favored a small encyclopedia for each state, which would contain essays on its history, education, agriculture, industry, and topography. Kellock preferred a volume concentrating on tourist routes with a brief background of the state. Alsberg's view assumed that the staff would write primarily for *readers;* Kellock's, that their audience was *tourists.* The compromise was a guide beginning with a variety of essays followed by comprehensive tour descriptions.[2]

Between January 1937, when the first state guide—*Idaho: A Guide in Word and Picture,* edited by Vardis Fisher—appeared, and 1942, when *Oklahoma: A Guide to the Sooner State,* the last, was published, FWP workers followed this model and compiled guides to all forty-eight states, Alaska, the District of Columbia, and various regions, cities, and locales.

The rationale for the guides was ex-

Entrance to the Indian Building, next to the railroad station, Albuquerque, New Mexico, early 1900s. Passengers were funneled between "live" Indians on the platform into the building's museum room, which displayed fine examples of Indian and Hispanic arts. Whittemann Collection, Prints and Photographs Division, Library of Congress

pressed by Alsberg in a letter to New Mexico state FWP director Ina Sizer Cassidy on May 13, 1936. Alsberg notes that Europeans have promoted their countries for the last two hundred years and that Americans go abroad to spend money.

The American Guide and the subsidiary local guides are designed by the U.S. government to teach both our travelers and travelling foreigners that we have many things worth seeing on this side of the Atlantic. If the guides keep some of the American millions, normally spent abroad, right here and add to them some of the European millions, which do not normally come here, they will do much to alleviate financial conditions in this country and reduce unemployment—and this in addition to what the Federal Writers' Projects are doing directly [primarily in hiring].

He goes on to remind Cassidy that "no part of the country will benefit more from the influence of the guides than will your part, since you live in one of the most interesting sections of the United States and increased travel will do much to put your unemployed in the way of finding permanent work." [3]

National tour editor Katherine Kellock "insisted that the guides satisfy all travelers, whether drivers on interstate highways or hardy trail explorers, and that they cover every mile of the country." Wishing to depart from the model of the Baedeker European guidebooks, with their loop tours from capital cities, she chose instead the north-to-south and east-to-west standard used by airlines and compass-oriented maps.[4] The 1938 official handbook for New Mexico FWP workers announced: "This Guide will be vastly more elaborate and detailed than any guide hitherto published by a firm or City. No section of the State is to be neglected by the Guide."

National officials stressed meticulous, comprehensive, accurate coverage and an entertaining style. Manuscript copy for tours was returned to Santa Fe from Washington on April 22, 1936, with the criticism: "We also feel that ... there is a tendency to write about the Points of Interest from a remote viewpoint whereas the tourist will read the Guide material on the spot. Consequently, care should be taken to convey the impression made on the tourist and to lead him around from point to

A highway sign in Datil, New Mexico, points the way to both natural wonders and such tourist necessities as Kodak film. (USF33-12829-M5) Photograph by Russell Lee, July 1940. Farm Security Administration Collection, Library of Congress

point." This "impression" had been explained by Alsberg in a January 17, 1936, letter to Cassidy: "We are particularly interested in scenic or human interest subjects—traditions, folklore, oldest settlers, ghost stories—anything that can be visualized as a halo to illuminate some objects which travelers can gaze on with horror or delight or some other form of emotion."

Alsberg again emphasized the concern for compelling style in a letter to acting New Mexico FWP director Aileen O'Bryan Nusbaum on June 13, 1939:

Try to make the readers see the white midsummer haze, the dust that rises in unpaved New Mexico streets, the slithery red earth roads of winter, the purple shadows of later afternoon, the brilliant yellow of autumn foliage against brilliant blue skies, the pseudo-cowboys in the tourist centers, the blank-faced Indians who are secretly amused by white antics, the patched and irregular walls of the older adobes; make him understand the social cleavages and jealousies, the strangely rotarianized "Indian dances," the life of the transplanted Oklahomans, Texans, Mexicans, Greenwich Villagers, and so on.

A letter of July 20 reiterates this request, pleading that "we want the type of visual description that Steinbeck would give—that is, descriptions of the types of buildings common to smaller New Mexican towns, mention of color, smells, sounds, signs, and above all, of the types of people seen along the streets." By then, Idaho novelist and FWP state director Vardis Fisher had been in Santa Fe for two weeks, helping Nusbaum finish the tours for the state guide. He answered Alsberg on July 24, 1939: "Nobody knows any better than I how thin some of these are; but it is impossible at this late stage to give them the Steinbeck color and details asked for . . . [because] the person or persons who logged under Mrs. Cassidy did a rotten job of it— a job so bad that it is almost beyond belief."

Twenty-five automobile tours appear in *New Mexico: A Guide to the Colorful State,* which was published by the New York firm of Hastings House in August 1940 and marketed for $2.50 a copy. The subtitle had been problematic, according to

Postcard from the Fred Harvey Hotels. The caption reads:

From the wheat fields of Kansas to the orange groves of California, the transcontinental highways which follow the popular "Sante Fe Route" traverse a region rich in scenic interest. . . . Along the way Fred Harvey Hotels provide convenient stops for meals and lodging and ideal headquarters for information concerning interesting journeys "off the beaten path."

Cafe and filling station on U.S. Highway 66, east of Albuquerque, New Mexico, July 1940. (LC-USF34-37074-D) Photograph by Russell Lee, Farm Security Administration Collection, Library of Congress

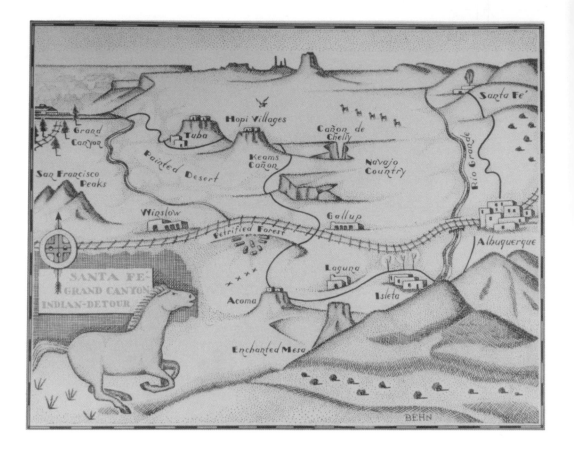

Charles Ethrige Minton, who oversaw final details on the book in his capacity as state director of what had after August 1939 become known as the Writers' Program of the reorganized WPA. Minton wrote national Writers' Program director John D. Newsom on May 20, 1940: "The subtitle 'A Guide to the Colorful State' was our own designation. There is no official State Name, and we found at least eight names that have been applied, such as 'Sunshine State,' 'Cactus State,' and so on, each worse than the other; so, because it is the most colorful of all the states in various ways, we decided on that subtitle, although we don't think it especially good."

The choice proved significant because the "colorful" designation distinguishes New Mexico's guide from all others, many of which characterize their states with epithets derived from physical features, flora, fauna, history, or inhabitants. Thus, Florida is "Southern-most," Maine "Down East," and Vermont the "Green Mountain State."

Flora are represented by sunflowers (Kansas), magnolias (Mississippi), and bluegrass (Kentucky), while Michigan is the "Wolverine State" and Wisconsin the "Badger State." Delaware is the "First State," California "Golden," and Oregon simply "End of the Trail." Iowans are "Hawkeyes." Only New Mexico's guide suggests a "folk" cast to the state's "colorful" natural wonders, history, and folklore/life, particularly the latter.

On December 10, 1935, public school educator Nina Otero-Warren and University of New Mexico president James F. Zimmerman submitted one of the first proposals for the study of folklore by the Federal Writers' Project. They suggested that the Southwest (New Mexico, Arizona, and southern California) be singled out for an organized collecting project that would in-

clude folktales, pioneer stories, cowboy songs, Spanish ballads, folk drama, and place names. They maintained that in New Mexico and the United States:

There was a time when standardization was rampant and all efforts, social and economic, converged on the idea of making the country uniform to the point where Southwestern villages would be identical to Middletown. Our art, our literature, and our music became one. Since then, however, we have become more appreciative of the differences in the various localities of the United States. In fact, we welcome a genuine distinction as something that should be preserved. The more genuine manifestation of true regional culture is embodied in the folklore production throughout the United States. The Southwest with its triple culture: Indian, Spanish, and English, offers a field to the sociologist, ethnologist, and the writer that no other part of America has to offer.

Otero-Warren and Zimmerman's proposal was not acted on directly in the region, but it clearly influenced the essay on folklore in the first section of *New Mexico: A Guide to the Colorful State.*

The folklore chapter for the New Mexico guide was pronounced "well-written" and "print-ready" copy by FWP editor Harold Rosenberg on March 29, 1938. Santa Fe editors and state director Ina Sizer Cassidy had revised three previous drafts in 1936 and 1937. The earlier versions—written by University of New Mexico students Robert Young and Eustaquio Garcia and checked by Modern Language Department faculty members T. M. Kercheville and Arthur L. Campa—had been criticized in Washington by FWP folklorists John A. Lomax and Benjamin A. Botkin, both of whom insisted on a balanced coverage of the state's three cultures. As associate FWP director George Cronyn wrote Cassidy on February 24, 1937: "I am returning the Folklore material with the comments of Mr. Lomax, who still is dissatisfied with the general structure and treatment of the essay. The material in your project work, and the character of it, was of such interest that we are very anxious to make this an outstanding essay."

The essay opens with examples of "un-

FIESTAS FOR 1940
MAY 3rd. SANTA CRUZ DAY
JUNE 13th. SAN ANTONIO DAY
JUNE 24th. SAN JUAN DAY
JULY 25th. AND 26th. SANTIAGO
SANTA ANNA, TAOS FIESTA DAYS.
AUG. 10. SAN LORENZO DAY.
SEPT. 28-29 & 30 SAN GERONIMO FIESTA

PARKING

Resting in the shade on Fiesta Day, Taos, New Mexico, July 1940. An article in New Mexico Magazine *for that year reads: "Particularly in the off-the-beaten-path towns of New Mexico will the visitor see little fiestas, processions, saint's day celebrations and folk festival presentations that are unique in all America." (USF33-12847) Photograph by Russell Lee, Farm Security Administration Collection, Library of Congress*

written" Indian myths and tales, noting that "in detail these mythic beliefs vary from tribe to tribe, and yet throughout the land occupied by the Pueblo and Navaho Indians there are fundamental similarities and uniformities that afford a basis of thought for a lore of a grandeur and beauty comparable to the great myths of the world." The writers claim that among the descendants of the "Spanish Colonists . . . may be found vigorous remains of sixteenth and seventeenth century folklore . . . [including] the philosophy of the common people . . . in the old *proverbios* or proverbs, similar to those Cervantes put in the mouth of Sancho Panza." Finally,

the coming of Americans from the East introduced new elements into the already rich

folk legendry. They brought a more vivid point of view and traditions that had their origins in other frontier regions. There were the buffalo hunters, the desert rats, and the cowboys. Folk tales concerning the adventures of early explorers and mountain men and Indian scouts who charted the wilderness sprang up almost overnight. . . .

In more recent times an interesting source of folk stories has been New Mexico's bad men—Billy the Kid, Black Jack Ketchum, "Buckshot" Roberts, Tom O'Foliard, and other gun-fighters of the territorial days, when many men acted on the theory that "the law didn't come west of the Pecos." . . .

Tales of the cattle trails in the Staked Plains country, of early ranchmen and railroaders, help to swell the volume of New Mexico folklore. Though many collections of cowboy and ranch, of Spanish and Indian folklore have been published, there is still a vast fund of material yet to be recorded.[5]

The influence of the 1935 Otero-Warren/Zimmerman proposal is also evident in the first essay of the 1940 state guide, "The State Today," virtually a paean to its colorfulness:

New Mexico today represents a blend of three cultures—Indian, Spanish, and American—each of which has had its time upon the stage and dominated the scene. The composite of culture which now, in the union of statehood, presents a harmonious picture upon casual inspection, is deceptive, for the veneer of Americanization in places runs thin indeed. It is difficult to think of a modern America in a village of Pueblo Indians, while the inhabitants dance for rain. To be sure, a transcontinental train may thunder by, or an airplane soar overhead; but the prayers never stop, the dance goes on, and the fantastic juxtaposition seems to widen the gap between. Who could dream of the American Way in a mountain hamlet where the sound of the Penitente flute is heard above the thud of the scourges, and Spanish-American villagers perform medieval rites of redemption in Holy Week?

These are extremes of incongruity, but they are true. They diminish in the vicinity of the larger towns and cities and vanish altogether in some places; but their existence, strong or weak, colors the contemporary scene. . . .

The interaction of the diverse elements of the population is slowly working toward homogeneity, dominated more and more by the irresistible middle current of Anglo-American civilization and the modern American tempo.[6]

And yet, the anonymous writers proclaim four paragraphs later, "homogeneous, New Mexico is not." North-central New Mexico is Spanish, northeastern Anglo from the Santa Fe Trail days, east-central and southeastern "markedly Texan in character," south-central settled by people from the Mississippi Valley, and northwestern, Mormon and Navajo. They end with the remarkable assertion that: "Suddenly and without forewarning, from almost any point in the State, one may step from modern America into Old Spain, or into aboriginal Indian territory, within the space of a few miles, just as one passes from an almost tropic climate into an arctic one, due to the many abrupt transitions from plain to plateau, up mountains and down again."

These "fantastic juxtapositions" and "abrupt transitions" echo Otero-Warren and Zimmerman's 1935 assertion:

There is a group of society that is fairly uniform throughout America. This group wears the same brand of shoes, eats the same foods, sings the same songs, and dances to the same music, throughout the nation. For this reason, this group is of less interest to the ethnologist. It is a person who is a product of the soil; who lives closely to it, that is able to give us the regional and varied aspect of America. Sophisticates at times try to imitate the Southwestern cowboy or the Indian, but because of the lack of sincerity the result is usually ridiculous. We are not trying to maintain a ridiculous civilization. . . . This is the true America that lies hidden in the Southwest, and this is the place where a collection of material which will lead us to understand these people lies ready for the folklorist, ethnologist, and anthropologist.

It also was ready for discovery by both residents and tourists during the 1940 Coronado Cuarto Centennial, a statewide commemoration that Erna Fergusson calls "such a world's fair as had never been known."

Publication of *New Mexico: A Guide to the Colorful State* was sponsored by the Coronado Cuarto Centennial Commission and the University of New Mexico. The requisite "Calendar of Annual Events" (seven pages) at the front of the book is followed by a special, three-page "Coronado Cuarto Centennial Folk Festival Calendar (Giving Principal Events from May 15 to November 1940)" and a single-page listing of dates for eleven New Mexico, four Texas, and two Arizona productions of the "Coronado Entrada (Full length historical play by Thomas Wood Stevens depicting incidents in Coronado's Expedition of 1540)." The latter required elaborate costuming for some five hundred participants, drawn from the local populace, whose pantomime of eighteen scenes on a stage the size of a football field was narrated by professional actors.

In 1931 Roswell schoolteacher Charles M. Martin had formally proposed a four-hundredth anniversary celebration honoring Coronado in order to give national currency to New Mexico history and to the Spanish Southwest. In 1935 Governor Clyde Tingley signed a legislative act creating the Coronado Cuarto Centennial Commission with University of New Mexico president James F. Zimmerman as chair. By adding Arizona, Texas, Colorado, Kansas, and Oklahoma to the plans, they were able to obtain two hundred thousand dollars in federal funds in 1939, when a United States Coronado Exposition Committee was established.

Albuquerque writer Erna Fergusson, who had formerly supervised training of Indian Detour Couriers, served on the New Mexico commission. She notes that "the first problem was how to make the uninformed aware of Coronado and of his importance" and that it was resolved by presenting the elaborate, dramatic Entradas scripted by Thomas Wood Stevens. The second problem involved "folk festivals":

Most of us live in small towns, making a living from farms or herds or unimportant jobs; most of our towns did not care for anything as elaborate or as costly as the Coronado Entrada. Many of our people can claim no descent from the conquerors. New Mexico has been made, too, by later comers of many stocks with a history and traditions quite as interesting if not quite as picturesque as the story of the conquerors. A Cuarto Centennial which did not take account of all this would fail of its intent to be an all-New Mexican fiesta. Every town, however small, should have a chance to present its history, to stage its typical show—rodeo, fair, religious feast, or celebration of legendary hero. . . . More than fifty small towns have received aid from the Cuarto Centennial Commission in putting on Coronado fiestas which vary from old Spanish morality plays to ballad contests, old fiddlers' tournaments, and revivals of forgotten dances. Generally these folk festivals are what has always been done. The effort has been to assist the townsfolk in advertising them for the benefit of visitors to New Mexico.[7]

The second problem was readily solved, Fergusson claims, because

the Southwest has so many feast days that its notable dates are days when nothing in particular is going on. In planning the Coronado Cuarto Centennial, it was necessary only to make a few adjustments in the regular sequence of gala events; to encourage every town to go on as it had been doing; to publish a calendar of festivities, and to declare the state "in fiesta." And there was such a world's fair as had never before been known.[8]

The automobile was the key to this massive promotion of ethnic tourism. In the conclusion to a 1938 booklet entitled *What the Coronado Cuarto Centennial Means to New Mexico,* the anonymous author claims: "If our many local celebrations are responsible for one car out of twenty remaining in the state one extra day, then the total increase in income from tourists should be between SEVEN AND EIGHT MILLION DOLLARS." Coronado Cuarto Centennial Commission publicist Edmund Sherman described what was to be done to ensure this windfall:

Every town in the State, too, will have some added interest. Those not listed for *Entradas* or folk festivals will have other types of celebrations such as rodeos, frontier days, old Trail days, local fiestas, county or local fairs, pageantry or cavalcades.

And, as always, at every Indian *pueblo* there will be dances on stated occasions. The holiday mood will prevail. Towns will be gaily decorated, and no village will be too small for a special celebration that will bring out the old time costumes and the native musicians with their fiddles and guitars to play the traditional dances *La Varsoviana* and *La Raspa* that today are as popular in the ball room as in the most isolated mountain village. There will be the folk plays, *Los Pastores, El Niño Perdido, Moros y Cristianos, Adan and Eva* which have been handed down orally from generation to generation. Coronado arts and crafts exhibits have been arranged at several points in the State. Virtually every activity of the summer, regular or special, will have some sort of tie-up with the Coronado celebration, whether it's conventions, coiffures, costumes, styles, sports, foods. Even tourists crossing the State in a few hours can hardly miss contact some way or other with the 400th anniversary celebration.[9]

The New Mexico Highway Department and the Tourist Bureau emphasized two names for the state in their 1930s promotions. *Roads to Cibola,* a thirty-two-page Highway Commission brochure, was published in 1931, and *Welcome to the Land of Enchantment,* a sixteen-page Tourist Bureau pamphlet, in 1937, the same year that "Land of Enchantment" first appeared on a road map. *Cibola* invokes images from the time of the Spanish conquistadors. The term *enchantment* is associated popularly with witchcraft and magic spells. But the Tourist Bureau personnel were influenced, apparently, by two publications: Lilian Whiting's 1906 travel book, *The Land of Enchantment: From Pike's Peak to the Pacific,* and Eugene Manlove Rhodes's 1911 short story, "A Number of Things." In both, "enchantment" is spectacle.

Whiting takes as her book's epigraph "The Fairest enchants me; / The Mighty commands me." She describes for the sightseer what she calls "four centres of sublime and unparalleled scenic sublimity which stand alone and unrivalled in the world"—in southern California, Arizona, Colorado, and New Mexico (primarily the environs of Santa Fe). Rhodes too relates enchantment to vision in "A Number of Things," his story describing the Socorro area of 1900:

A land of mighty mountains, far seen, gloriously tinted, misty opal, purple, blue and amethyst; a land of enchantment and mystery. Those same opalescent hills, seen closer, are decked with barbaric colors—reds, yellows or pinks, brown or green or gray; but, from afar, shapes and colors ebb and flow, altered daily, hourly, by subtle sorcery of atmosphere, distance and angle; deepening, fading, combining into new and fantastic forms and hues—to melt again as swiftly into others yet more bewildering.[10]

The experience of variable, visual "enchantment" is part of travel by foot, horseback, wagon, and automobile, *not* of rail travel. Like pre-rail methods of transportation, cars, which theoretically can be slowed, accelerated, turned, and stopped virtually at will, permit the "enchantment" of riders' vision. Drivers and passengers who must leave their vehicles to attend to physical needs are more likely to see and interact with people; passengers on a train or station platform are insulated from the passing scene.

Car travelers' interactions may or may not prove to be all the ethnic tourist seeks in getting "close to Nature's bosom" through "Peasant and Primitive peoples." This may in part account for why Edmund Sherman was at such pains to assure Coronado Cuarto Centennial tourists that wherever they went they would meet quaint and colorful celebrants, not indifferent or even hostile strangers.

Particularly in the off-the-beaten-path towns of New Mexico will the visitor see little *fiestas,* processions, saint's day celebrations and folk festival presentations that are unique in all America. Here the visitor will be carried back into history a century or two, or four, as traditional observances are carried on with all the simplicity and naturalness that is the heritage of these people who for four hundred years have tilled the soil in areas that have been almost untouched by modern civilization.[11]

The "true America that lies hidden" must also be a non-threatening America.

Early twentieth-century tourists to the Southwest were content to view the land and its denizens through the moving picture of the train window and in nearly zoo-like, stationside retail facilities and museums. By the 1920s, car-facilitated encounters were

Along the Apache Trail between Globe and Phoenix, Arizona, May 1940. The automobile allowed tourists the freedom to explore the region on their own, "off the beaten path," as Fred Harvey Indian Detours brochures put it. (LC-USF34-36183-D) Photograph by Russell Lee, Farm Security Administration Collection, Library of Congress

mediated by chauffeurs and hostess-guides on Indian Detours away from the tracks. Finally, as more and more people owned cars and felt free to strike out on their own, more and more of the region had to be validated as worthy of a sightseeing tour or at least armchair attention to its "local color." This was a primary task of federal workers on the American Guide Series. They and those associated with the Coronado Cuarto Centennial were attempting to create the sense of a benevolent, celebratory folklife for the whole region, thereby exhorting the ethnic tourist to experience a "colorful" state "more colorful than ever," for, "to happen upon one of these off-the-beaten path celebrations gives one the impression of having been the discoverer of something really new and different—yet these celebrations are as old as New Mexico." [12]

NOTES

1. Nelson H. H. Graburn, "Tourism: The Sacred Journey," in *Hosts and Guests: The Anthropology of Tourism,* ed. Valene Smith (Philadelphia: University of Pennsylvania Press, 1977), 26, 27.

The Atchison, Topeka & Santa Fe Railway began in Kansas in 1868, reached the New Mexico line in 1878, and established a West Coast connection in 1883. English immigrant Frederick Henry Harvey (1835–1901) opened his first railroad-connected lunchroom at Topeka in 1876 and later signed contracts with the Santa Fe to lease and operate all its food services (on trains and trackside), hotel accommodations, and other station facilities. James David Henderson, *"Meals by Fred Harvey": A Phenomenon of the American West* (Fort Worth: Texas Christian University Press, 1969). The Grand Canyon Railway, a subsidiary of the Santa Fe, made its inaugural run from Williams to the south rim on September 17, 1901. At the Grand Canyon, the Fred Harvey Company opened El Tovar Hotel (1905), Hopi House (1905), the Lookout (1914), Hermit's Rest (1914), Phantom Ranch at the bottom of the Canyon (1922), Hopi Watchtower (1932), Bright Angel Lodge (1935), and dormitories for employees in 1936 and 1937. Most of these structures, like many throughout the Santa Fe–Harvey system, were the work of Harvey Company architect and decorator Mary Elizabeth Jane Colter (1869–1958). J. Donald Hughes, *In the House of Stone and Light: A Human History of the Grand Canyon* (Grand Canyon Natural History Association, 1978); Virginia L. Grattan, *Mary Colter: Builder Upon the Red Earth* (Flagstaff, Arizona: Northland Press, 1980). *See also,* D. H. Thomas, *The Southwestern Indian Detours: The Story of the Fred Harvey/Sante Fe Railway experiment in "de-*

tourism" (Phoenix, Arizona: Hunter Publishing Co., 1978).

2. Monty Noam Penkower, *The Federal Writers' Project: A Study in Government Patronage of the Arts* (Urbana: University of Illinois Press, 1977), 31.

3. Quotations here and below are from FWP administrative documents in Washington, D.C., at the National Archives (Record Group 69) or/ and in Santa Fe, New Mexico, repositories at the History Library, Museum of New Mexico, or/and the New Mexico State Records Center and Archives. Because the manuscripts are not readily accessible, exact locations are not given.

4. Penkower, 85, 86.

5. *New Mexico: A Guide to the Colorful State,* compiled by Workers of the Writers' Program of the Work Projects Administration in the State of New Mexico (New York: Hastings House, 1940), 98, 100, 103–4, 106.

6. *New Mexico Guide,* 3.

7. Erna Fergusson, "The Coronado Cuarto Centennial," *New Mexico Quarterly* 10 (1940): 69.

8. Erna Fergusson, *Our Southwest* (New York: Alfred A. Knopf, 1940), 340.

9. Edmund Sherman, "New Mexico Celebrates," *New Mexico Magazine* (June 1940), 13, 15.

10. Lilian Whiting, *The Land of Enchantment: Notes from Pike's Peak to the Pacific* (Boston: Little, Brown, 1906), 3–4; Eugene Manlove Rhodes, "A Number of Things," *Saturday Evening Post,* April 8, 1911, reprinted in *The Rhodes Reader: Stories of Virgins, Villains, and Varmints,* selected by W. H. Hutchinson, 2d ed. (Norman: University of Oklahoma Press, 1975), 82.

11. Sherman, 12.

12. Sherman, 11, 12.

Old Men and New Schools

Rationalizing Change in the Southern Mountains

BY DAVID E. WHISNANT

Wilma Creech of Pine Mountain, Harlan County, Kentucky, on a mountain cabin front porch with a High Spinning Wheel. This and other photographs by Doris Ulmann, used in Allen Eaton's book Handicrafts of the Southern Highlands, *presented an old-fashioned image of country folk and rural simplicity. But the picture was staged by the photographer, and Creech donned a bonnet and dress and shed her shoes especially for it. Used with the special permission of Berea College and the Doris Ulmann Foundation*

When it comes to the popular image and understanding of the southern mountains, there is little that is new under the sun. The region gets rediscovered about once every generation. It happened first with the local color writers of the late nineteenth century, again in the 1920s and 1930s, and yet again during the War on Poverty and Great Society days of the 1960s.[1] The stories, images, metaphors, half-truths, and untruths associated with such rediscoveries have been retreaded and recirculated countless times.

Why such a patterned repetition has proved so durable for now over a century is complicated. What is reasonably clear is that the public political and cultural ritual associated with the process has deep roots both in the history of the region and in its interaction with national character and development. The patterns are rooted partly, for example, in the ethnocentrism of the local color writers who summered on the verandahs of mountain tourist hotels and returned to their New England homes to generalize broadly on "mountain people" for genteel, middle-class monthly maga-

zines.[2] Other roots have been nourished by the political ignorance, class bias, and cultural provincialism of mainstream America (especially as those traits were reflected in the mass media): it has always been easier to prattle about the "isolation" and "backwardness" of the mountains than to deal with the more complicated and threatening fact of their systematic colonization by northern-based corporations.[3] Nor can one overlook the importance of some *national* myths in periods of national anxiety (the nativistic years of the late nineteenth century, the Depression era, and the turbulent 1960s), when it proved comforting to "know" that no matter how unstuck things became elsewhere, all was as ever back in the hills.

But my purpose here is to unravel only one small strand of this complexly woven fabric of national myth and regional cultural history. Between about 1890 and the mid-1920s, a number of college-educated women from Bluegrass Kentucky and the Seven Sisters colleges* created and promoted the culturally and politically legitimizing myth of an aged mountaineer who implores them to do what they were in fact already disposed to do: start missionary schools for mountain children.[4] The women were often known in the mountains as "fotched-on," that is, brought in from somewhere outside.

I pick up the thread first in one of the most influential cultural/social documents on the region published during the 1930s: Allen Eaton's *Handicrafts of the Southern Highlands*. It was issued in 1937 by the Russell Sage Foundation, which had been funding and directing work in the mountains since pioneering sociologist John C. Campbell's social survey just after the turn of the century. Much of the appeal of Eaton's book derived from Doris Ulmann's photographs, with which it was illustrated. During the next half-century, those photographs (and many others by the same photographer) have been widely reproduced as authentic representations of isolated, picturesque, culturally conservative mountain

---

* Barnard, Bryn Mawr, Mount Holyoke, Radcliffe, Smith, Vassar, and Wellesley

few pages later, it was a family affair, as is evident in the photograph of Aunt Sal Creech and her husband Uncle William, who, Eaton tells us, a quarter of a century earlier had implored the "fotched-on" Bluegrass ladies Katherine Pettit and May Stone to come to Pine Mountain and start a school. As an inducement to the women, Uncle William donated over a hundred acres of land. Although Allen Eaton had far too much integrity to intentionally mislead his readers, it is nearly two hundred pages after the corn-grinding and wool-spinning photos that one encounters a brief account of how they were taken:

When Doris Ulmann went to Pine Mountain to procure the photographs for this book, several of the grandchildren and other members of the Creech family dressed in old costumes and were photographed at work as in pioneer days (Eaton, *Handicrafts*, p. 258).

So this is after all not a simple episode of cultural documentation; the barefoot corn-grinding and wool-spinning daughters are actually tertiary figures in a complex myth someone is at considerable pains to perpetuate. Uncle William turns out to be the principal figure in a myth about tradition and change, individuals and institutions, cultural preservation and revival, region and nation.

Pioneer cabin of William and Sal Creech. "Uncle" William Creech gave the land for the Pine Mountain Settlement School, and this log house, which he built, is now a local museum. Photograph by Doris Ulmann, used with the special permission of Berea College and the Doris Ulmann Foundation

people.[5] The idiom is familiar: slightly soft focus, sepia-toned prints, side or three-quarter views (perhaps to suggest the "natural" shyness and reticence of mountaineers), rustic settings, and hands at work producing supposedly traditional artifacts.

But to get closer to the pattern I am interested in here, consider two photographs of the Creech sisters of Harlan County, Kentucky. In the late 1930s, it must have reassured many a reader of Eaton's book to know that deep in at least a few Appalachian hollers, young women in bonnets and linsey-woolsey were still grinding corn and spinning wool by hand. Indeed, we learn a

While writing *All That Is Native and Fine* (1983), I pieced together the stories of two of the schools founded by fotched-on ladies. This experience taught me that Uncle William was but one of many such carefully packaged and perennially merchandised mythic figures. With surprising consistency, one mission and settlement school after another tied its local and larger public image to a legendary "old man of the mountains," in response to whose Macedonian call* the school was supposedly estab-

* Macedonia was a country to the north of Greece that Paul evangelized after a man from it pleaded, "Come over into Macedonia and help us." (Acts 16:9)

lished and through whose warrant it achieved part of its legitimacy both within and beyond the local community.

To Uncle William can be added immediately Uncle Luce Scroggs (whose plea lead to the John C. Campbell Folk School), Abisha Johnson (who reportedly implored Boston-born Alice Lloyd to come and start a school that would help his children live "not liken the hog but unliken the hog"), and no doubt others who have not yet come to my attention.[6] In photographs and books, schools and festivals, newspaper and magazine articles, novels and short stories, and eventually in small local museums, such figures were memorialized and institutionalized, and thus, at length, graven upon the public consciousness.

The earliest example I am aware of arose in connection with an embryonic social settlement established by Vassar graduate Susan G. Chester near Asheville, North Carolina, about 1894. Speaking to the Philadelphia Conference of Church Women in February 1893, Chester said that

In the mountains of western North Carolina three hundred thousand men and women are existing in total ignorance of *all* that serves to make *life really* worth living and seemingly devoid of a desire to rise above the level of the *animal*. . . .

Dark, far darker than I would willingly paint them, are the cabin homes of a vast number of mountaineers.[7]

To bring light into such awesome darkness, Chester proposed to establish a small church-related "college settlement," similar to those her classmates were establishing in both urban and rural areas elsewhere. Impressing upon her listeners the urgency of the task and the great good that might be done, she told how "one day in the autumn of '91 a shaggy bearded, loud-voiced almost savage-looking" mountaineer rode his mule twenty miles to a local clergyman's house in Asheville, tenderly carrying a shawl-wrapped "pale, delicate little girl whose labored breathing and the faraway look in [whose] blue eyes show that the world's trials are almost at an end for the poor little soul." In a choking voice the mountaineer says to the clergyman, "O, Mister, I've rid plumb twenty mile to see you'uns. They told me as how you knowed a powerful good man who'd make my little 'un well. I 'low his name is Mr. God. Whur d'ye reckon I can find Him?"

The motifs Chester enunciated were repeated countless times during the next twenty or thirty years as similar enterprises sprang up elsewhere in the mountains: the darkness and degradation of mountain life; the ignorance and guilelessness of mountain people; the special plight of mountain children (indeed the portrayal of all mountain people as children); the claims of conditions in the mountains upon the consciences of the fortunate and cultivated world beyond; the redemptive potential of the simple lived example; and the plaintive calls for help that echoed from distant coves and hollers.

Although Chester's shaggy mountaineer is not yet refined into the ideal type of an Uncle Sol or Uncle William, he is a recognizable prototype: an old mountain man who summons what limited wit he has and takes a long ride from a physically and spiritually darksome holler to bring his wasting child or grandchild to the light offered by the local agents of Mr. God. Over the next

forty years—from Chester's 1893 speech to Uncle Luce Scroggs's funeral at Brasstown, North Carolina, in 1935—that prototype was to be reworked and refined many times.

As I have come to recognize it in its fullest form (some versions emphasize certain elements more than others), the myth runs something like this: Conditions in the mountains are desperate and will never improve substantially in a natural or organic way because mountaineers lack the energy, initiative, resources, and vision to design a new world and bring it into being. Prospecting through the mountains for a place to induce desperately needed changes, one or two well-bred women (usually from beyond the mountains) are approached rather providentially by an old mountaineer who has heard of their mission. Having walked or ridden (usually a mule) some great distance (twenty miles seems about the mini-

The Pine Mountain Settlement School, near Harlan, Kentucky, August 1940. (LCUSF34-55848-D) Photograph by Marion Post Wolcott, Farm Security Administration Collection, Library of Congress

Uncle Luce Scroggs. Courtesy of the John C. Campbell Papers, Southern Historical Collection, University of North Carolina

mum to qualify), sometimes in poor clothing and/or bad weather, and sometimes bringing a winsome (or ailing) child or grandchild with him, he implores the women (in his picturesque mountain idiom) to take up residence and "help us pore people." Knowing he himself is too old to be helped much, he generally suggests setting up a school for the children (the "grands and greats"). As evidence of his trust and commitment, he gives a gift—money, usually, or land for the school. Moved by his entreaty and gift, the women comply. His example elicits similar commitment from the entire community. The school is built, becomes a beacon in the mountain darkness, and both transforms individual lives and provides a model for the new social order. In due time, the old mountaineer's cabin is moved to the school grounds to serve as a museum of the old ways that paradoxically both died to give birth to the new school and found a new life in its programs.

It does not take much imagination, or much acquaintance with the world's sacred and secular literatures, to recognize that one is dealing here only partially with actual historical events. The story is profoundly resonant.

A relatively spare version appears in a short story White Top Folk Festival organizer Annabel Morris Buchanan wrote in the 1930s, "Moses Asks for a Sign."[8] In the story, three sophisticated cultural workers are having an evening conversation before a fire in a cabin on White Top mountain in southwest Virginia. "We've got to get away from it," says one—a dramatist. "This is the age of machinery against the folk. We must find some way to re-create the old folk life, get back to simplicity of thought and beliefs . . . or else, be crushed under the weight of our own machinery." Their perplexity is evidently shared by their mountain neighbors, for in the midst of a storm Brother Moses, a bearded itinerant mountain preacher "famous for his simple faith" stumbles into the cabin. "We come before Thee," he prays, "groping for the truth. Reveal . . . Thy way to us pore, ignorant children."

Not surprisingly, the distinction between God and the three sophisticates is not sharply drawn in the story. They are sure that the truth they have is the truth Brother Moses seeks, and that its power for redemptive personal and social change is great. "Before our eyes," the story continues, "the ignorant mountain preacher became transformed into a being of dignity, power, and exaltation, the mouthpiece of the mountain folk." Buchanan's own institutional mechanism for bringing light and truth was the White Top Folk Festival, which selected and promoted nationally a rather exotic version of local musical culture designed to stem what the festival organizers considered to be a rising tide of tawdry commercial hillbilly music.[9]

More elaborate versions of the myth came to be associated with Hindman and Pine Mountain settlement schools, and with the John C. Campbell Folk School. The Campbell school version focused on Uncle Luce Scroggs. As the story was told by Mrs. Campbell after his death in 1935, Scroggs came with a group of neighbors to ask her and Marguerite Butler for "a school which will help the country, not just make preachers and teachers." "It was Uncle Luce," Mrs. Campbell said, who was "first to beg for a school. It was Uncle Luce and his family who gave us our first 25 acres of land; it was Uncle Luce who followed every development of the School with keenest interest. . . ."[10]

Scroggs was mentor and friend, guide and inspiration, "link between the old and the new in the mountains." When he died, Mrs. Campbell wrote, "friends passed around the casket, the birds sang overhead and the great pine tree never ceased its soughing. [Following the casket] in single file, [we] wended our way down one path and up again, twisting back and down, along the highway and up the hill to the old home. Silently it moved, on and on, seemingly without end." And when Doris Ulmann came to the school the next year to make her photographs, some of her subjects (along with folk school woodcarvers and weavers) were Uncle Luce's grandchildren.[11]

More elaborate yet is the oft-told story of Pine Mountain Settlement School's Uncle William Creech (1845–1918), a late, brief version of which is in Allen Eaton's book. As former Pine Mountain head Glyn Morris noted forty years after the Creech story first appeared, Uncle William and Aunt Sal are "mythical characters out of a misty past."[12] Most of the elements are there: a little cabin up a narrow creek amidst giant poplars, old man (Civil War veteran, father of nine children, grandfather of many), small learning, hard work, dim prospects for a better life. But a preacher brings word of some women who aim to start a school. Creech writes them an imploring letter; they visit; he gives 135 acres "to be used for school purposes as long as the Constitution of the United States stands, Hopin' it may make a bright and intelligent people after I'm dead and gone."

An interesting extension of the Creech myth was related by Samuel and Nola Vander Meer more than twenty years after Creech issued the call for Pettit to come to Pine Mountain. As the Vander Meers tell it, Presbyterian mountain missionary Mary Rose McCord had been working in the North Carolina mountains for about fifteen years. She decides to move to Kentucky, but is uncertain about which community to choose. "At Pine Mountain," the Vander Meers relate, "the Lord's prospector [Miss McCord] found Uncle William Creech. Telling him of her quandry, she received the answer: 'Go to Cutshin. For a long time they've wanted me and Katherine and Ethel there, but we've got too much to do here. But you must go,—they need you on Cutshin Creek.'" She goes and "at the county seat found one who seemed to be waiting for an answer to his prayers."[13]

So far as I know, the most elaborate, durable, and widely disseminated version of the myth surrounds Hindman Settlement School's Uncle Sol Everidge. Although it appeared in many forms during the school's early years, the most accessible version is in William Aspenwall Bradley's *Scribner's Magazine* article of 1918. Bradley said Uncle Sol "wore homespun trousers and a white home-woven shirt of flax . . . [and] his heels were so hard he could crush chestnuts out of the burr without feeling it." For the rest, his aspect was patriarchal and imposing. He was tall, straight, and still strong. He had a massive head, with thick, white hair and heavy eyebrows, under which his fine dark eyes shone out with an expression of remarkable intelligence and nobility.

"When I was jest a chuck of a boy . . . ," he said, "and hoein' corn on the steep mountainside, I'd look up Troublesome [Creek] and down Troublesome, and wonder if anybody'd ever come in and larn us anything. But nobody ever come in, and nobody ever went out, and we jest growed up and never knowed nothin'. I never had a chanst to larn anything myself, but I got chillern and grandchillern jest as bright as other folkses', and I want 'em to have a chanst. . . ."

"Times is a-gittin' wuss and wuss," he continued. "When I was a boy I was purty bad. The next gineration was wusser." Then, pointing to a baby whose mother . . . was fanning it with a white turkey wing, he asked, "What will this gineration be unless you women come to Hindman and help us?"

Once spread abroad, the image proved

remarkably attractive and durable. A picture of Uncle Sol—sitting in a split-bottomed chair in an open cabin doorway, barefoot, with rolled-up trouser legs—graced scores of Hindman Settlement School brochures, appeared in countless newspaper articles and magazine stories, and was reproduced on a brochure announcing a Hindman benefit performance of Lula Vollmer's play *Sun-Up* in Chicago in 1923. The story was repeated in May Stone's 1928 sketch of Uncle Sol in *Mountain Life and Work,* in Pauline Ritchie Kermiet's memorial article on one of the school's founders, May Stone, in 1946 (Kermiet was one of Uncle Sol's "greats"), in a Bryn Mawr College thesis of 1975, in both the local *Troublesome Creek Times* and the state-regional *Louisville Courier-Journal* in 1980, and in the Appalachian Regional Commission's public relations magazine in 1981. Uncle Sol's cabin was long ago moved to the school grounds and reconstructed, where it remains as a memorial more than eighty years after his fabled barefoot walk to Hindman.

Although the story varies slightly from one account to another, it has the shape of a myth whose essential features have long since been agreed upon. The consensus was and is that Uncle Sol was the "visionary founder" of the school, as Pauline Ritchie Kermiet called him.

From Bradley's account one may begin to understand how the myth was tailored to the *Scribner's* audience, and therefore how it may have helped to control aspects of the ritual of interaction between such people—amongst whom Katherine Pettit campaigned annually for money for her school. Bradley said that Pettit first came to eastern Kentucky out of "pure curiosity," stirred by accounts of the mountain feuds that were quite unaccountably raging amongst "Americans of unimpeachable pedigree, descendents of pioneer woodsmen and Revolutionary soldiers speaking the language of Shakespeare and singing ballads straight from the pages of Percy's *Reliques.* . . ." On their visit, Bradley said, the "women of the rich and aristocratic Blue Grass" heard the call from Uncle Sol. "It had never occurred to them before," he reported, "that they

might do anything to alleviate the poverty and suffering that so appalled them." Their "idle curiosity" was "suddenly transformed" into a desire to help. Moved by Uncle Sol's request, the women went about their task protected from violence by a dozen armed men who "accompanied them everywhere."

Thus to Bradley and his *Scribner's* readers, Uncle Sol was—wondrously—an idealistic and progressive hillbilly, barefoot and ignorant himself, of course, but admirably ambitious for his multigenerational progeny. And probably most important, he bore the simple message that a convulsed region and an increasingly uncertain nation wanted to hear: The ills attending rapid economic and social change could be healed by "education"—conventionally conceived and individually administered. One comes to understand this truth, moreover, not as a result of historical, economic, social, or cultural analysis, but in the midst of one's essential innocence, guided and transformed by a fortuitous encounter of rather scriptural sonority.

But why has the myth of Uncle Sol (and by implication, those of the other "uncles," as well), so marketable from the 1890s to the 1920s to a large but rather specialized audience, proven so durable and so much more widely saleable for what will soon be a hundred years?

Uncle Sol was, first of all, both an immediately recognizable regional stereotype and a perennially attractive national archetype. He was a regional and national patriarch (conveniently named Solomon), hallowed ancestor redivivus, redemptive apparition from our mythic past. He was both Natty Bumppo and the biblical Moses who crossed the mountains and saw a promised land a-borning for his children at the fortuitously named "Forks of Troublesome" (creek). Nearly thirty years later May Stone recalled that Uncle Sol's reddish-brown eyes "were those of a seer and prophet, one who had seen much and dreamed of much unseen." [14]

Thus in Uncle Sol were blended classic elements of American values, social and political views, and regional prejudices. He promised a solution that entailed no social cost, that confirmed rather than challenged the status quo. Hence the myth was useful each time the nation had to face once again the embarrassing anomaly of what one television network documentary of the 1960s called "rich land and poor people."

In 1895 when Katherine Pettit made her first reconnoitering visit to eastern Kentucky and met Uncle Sol, after all, the virgin forests were already falling beneath the loggers' axes, and by 1913, when she departed Hindman for Uncle William's Pine Mountain, the newly opened eastern Kentucky coalfields were booming. When Uncle Luce told Mrs. Campbell he and his folks wanted the school she wanted to start, juke boxes were being installed at the drugstore in nearby Murphy, Douglas Fairbanks was on the silver screen at the new movie theater, and the Hiwassee was being dammed to send electricity to the new electric refrigerators the local newspaper was advertising. But the several hoary "Uncles" nevertheless came walking in from afar, miraculously untouched by the surrounding environmental and social holocaust,[15] saying that the past was still alive back in there, and that the problems we have out here won't cost much to fix—either in money or in painful re-evaluation of regional patterns or national priorities.

Conveniently, Uncle Sol, Uncle Luce, "Moses," Uncle William, and the rest turn out to be both strong proponents of progress and determined conservators of the past: walking, talking, reassuring guarantors that stable past and dynamic future could coexist. In her memorial article on Uncle Luce, Mrs. Campbell said "no one recognized more keenly the need for change" than he, but that one of his greatest interests was the folk museum that was being erected at the school in his memory. A captioned photograph in the article showed Uncle Luce with "his shining gray head bent over the making of puncheon steps" for the museum.[16] Similarly, we are told that Uncle William Creech was both the earliest exponent of rotating crops in his area, and the staunchest defender of the old ways. "Today his home is still a thoroughly old-fashioned one," Pine Mountain teacher Ethel DeLong reported,

Uncle Luce Scroggs's cabin reconstructed as a museum at the John C. Campbell Folk School. Courtesy of the John C. Campbell Papers, Southern Historical Collection, University of North Carolina

where the coal oil lamps have never superseded the pine faggots, and where the hackle, loom, and reel are kept and loved, while . . . his wife . . . wears a red bandana over her head after the old custom. . . . There is a fine atmosphere of courtesy and high-mindedness in the home.[17]

Moreover, the Uncle Sol/William/Luce figure resonated *across* the cultural boundaries that separated the Seven Sisters colleges or the Bluegrass from Knott County or Buncombe County. Fotched-on women might be (as in the title of Lucy Furman's widely read novel of 1923) "quare" indeed to mountain people, as most mountaineers were to *Scribner's* readers, but Moses was as familiar to both as last Sunday's sermon, and an "old man of the mountains" was a smooth-worn and congenial image. The metaphor of a long walk across the mountains was also expressive to both groups at many levels. To the urban audience it im-

Reconstructing part of the cabin museum at the John C. Campbell Folk School, July 1936. Courtesy of the John C. Campbell Papers, Southern Historical Collection, University of North Carolina

of what they did, they *were* "fotched-on," many of them—"quare women" who weren't married and didn't have children, who had been to college, rode horseback by themselves through the mountains, and had strange ideas about how folks should cook, clothe themselves, celebrate holidays, and raise their children. The women's grounds for legitimacy were therefore narrowly bounded culturally, and a warrant (or presumed warrant) from the immediate community was useful both within and beyond the mountains. After their initial visit to the isolated town of Hindman (the railroad was not to arrive for another dozen years), Pettit and Stone returned with some potential financial backers to assess possibilities for starting a school. "They said that after travelling forty miles on horseback from the railroad to reach Hindman," May Stone recalled,

it did not seem very practical to start a school. . . . [But] . . . the sight of Uncle Solomon, sitting in a chair at the front of the courthouse and talking of the future of the young people, was sufficient inspiration to make any one feel a slacker who would hesitate to respond.[18]

It may indeed not be too far-fetched to suggest that the sundry uncles were surrogate fathers for a generation of women testing their own independence for the first time. It is no news, after all, that Victorian business and professional men were not necessarily ideal fathers for their newly liberated, college-educated, professionally ambitious, socially conscious daughters.[19] If one wished to read the myth as a modern psychological narrative, one might see Uncle Sol's walk as having taken him not from a darksome holler to the Forks of Troublesome, but from the deepest recesses of Katherine Pettit's and May Stone's minds into the forefront of their consciousness. And the message he brought was not "come over and help us pore, ignorant people live not liken the hog but unliken the hog." It was instead "I bestow my blessing, daughter, upon you and upon what you are doing." The "uncles" bestowed what was then at once a psychological, familial, social, cultural, ethical, and political warrant.

plied that old ways could and should be left, that the ways of the fotched-on women were superior, but also that the old ways were admirable to an extent and might be made the substructure of new institutions that formally celebrated tradition while they molded mountain boys and girls in distinctly new images. To mountaineers, on the other hand, the walk bespoke the hardiness and fortitude of mountain people, and the final falsity of certain aspects of the stereotype.

And finally, I suspect, the myth was *useful* to the settlement women, not only socially and politically because it communicated across those boundaries of class and culture but also personally and psychologically because it assuaged some of the women's own doubts and uncertainties. However one may feel about the legitimacy

A final tentative suggestion: Years of studying social change institutions in the mountains have taught me that much of their history—if it is ever to be adequately described—must be dealt with at the intimate, interpersonal level. Unfortunately, that level is difficult and delicate to document and explore.[20] I am nevertheless confident that in the cases being considered here, interpersonal and institutional histories are exquisitely intertwined. In the John C. Campbell correspondence, for example, a number of letters suggest growing problems between Katherine Pettit and May Stone at Hindman prior to Pettit's departure to start the new Pine Mountain Settlement School in 1913. Finally, in May of that year, Campbell wrote to John Glenn of the Russell Sage Foundation, "I am happy to say that Miss Pettit's departure to Pine Mountain is regarded simply as a necessary move because of the growth of the school. . . . I was very anxious to have that

go out as a correct impression, and wrote Miss Pettit about it several years ago."[21]

How much interpersonal history is buried in those cryptic comments we will probably never know. What is clear, however, is that that particular truth—along with others that were larger and still more complicated—was shrouded and packaged in the story of old Uncle William Creech. Like bonnets and granny dresses, the Appalachian uncles' story could be shaken out and photographed at will for a public to which some truths were more palatable than others. Between the 1890s and the 1980s—from the time Susan Chester told it to the Philadelphia church women in order to move them to Christian philanthropy until it appeared in the public relations magazine of the federal Appalachian Regional Commission as a justification for certain aspects of economic development policy—it was a familiar item in the elaborately ritualized interaction between region and nation.

1. These episodes of Appalachian history are explored in David E. Whisnant, *Modernizing the Mountaineer: People, Power, and Planning in Appalachia* (Boone, N.C.: Appalachian Consortium Press, 1980).

2. *See* Henry D. Shapiro, *Appalachia on Our Mind: The Southern Mountains and Mountaineers in the American Consciousness, 1870–1920* (Chapel Hill: University of North Carolina Press, 1978).

3. For an account of the industrialization process, *see* Ronald D. Eller, *Miners, Millhands, and Mountaineers: Industrialization of the Appalachian South, 1880–1930* (Knoxville: University of Tennessee Press, 1982).

4. The existence of such a pattern of mythicized figures was first pointed out, so far as I know, by Helen Lewis, Sue Kobak, and Linda Johnson in their essay in Jim Axelrod, ed., *Growin' Up Country* (Clintwood, Va.: Council of the Southern Mountains, 1973), 140.

5. Jonathan Williams, ed., *The Appalachian Photographs of Doris Ulmann* (Penland, N.C.: Jargon Society, 1971).

6. William S. Dutton, *Stay On, Stranger* (New York: Farrar, Straus, and Young, 1954), 18. No "uncle" figures turned up in connection with a similar but earlier school founded among people whose culture was *not* romantically valorized by the northern missionaries who founded it (the Penn School established during the Civil War for the Gullah-speaking blacks of South Carolina's Sea Islands). *See* Elizabeth Jacoway, *Yankee Missionaries in the South: The Penn School Experiment* (Baton Rouge: Louisiana State University Press, 1980).

7. Susan G. Chester, "College Settlements and Their Relation to the Church," [Philadelphia] *Church Standard*, June 17, 1893, 14–15. Mission schools had been established in the mountains as early as the 1840s. *See* Susan Fenimore Cooper, ed., *William West Skiles: A Sketch of Missionary Life at Valle Crucis in Western North Carolina, 1842–1862* (New York: James Pott & Co, 1890).

8. Annabel Morris Buchanan Papers, Southern Historical Collection, University of North Carolina.

9. An extended analysis of the White Top Folk Festival appears in David E. Whisnant, *All That Is Native and Fine: The Politics of Culture in an American Region* (Chapel Hill: The University of North Carolina Press, 1983), 181–252.

10. Olive Dame Campbell, Scroggs obituary article in John C. Campbell Folk School newsletter no. 18, November 1935. See *Mountain Life and Work* 11 (January 1936):10–11 for Doris Ulmann's photographs of Scroggs and his wife.

11. The photographs of the Scroggs grandchildren appeared in the John C. Campbell Folk School newsletter no. 19, May 1936, p. 2. Glyn Morris, *Less Travelled Roads* (New York: Vantage Press, 1977), 81, reprints an account (possibly by Ethel DeLong) of forty mountain men carrying Uncle William's coffin through the hills for burial—an account that echoes elements of Uncle Luce Scroggs's cortege as described by Mrs. Campbell. A longer version of the Campbell folk school story is to be found in Whisnant, *All That Is Native and Fine*, 103–80.

12. Morris, *Less Travelled Roads*, 75–82.

13. Eaton, *Handicrafts of the Southern Highlands*, 216, 175, 68; Samuel and Nola Vander Meer, "Crooked Paths and Straight Men," *Mountain Life and Work* 11 (April 1935): 5–7.

14. *Mountain Life and Work* 4 (April 1928): 17.

15. Readers who wish details on these widespread patterns of destruction and their attendant social costs may consult Helen M. Lewis, et al., *Colonialism in Modern America: The Appalachian Case* (Boone, N.C.: Appalachian Consortium Press, 1978); John Gaventa, *Power and Powerlessness: Quiescence and Rebellion in an Appalachian Valley* (Urbana: University of Illinois Press, 1980); and Ronald D. Eller, *Miners, Millhands and Mountaineers: Industrialization of the Appalachian South, 1880–1930* (Knoxville: University of Tennessee Press, 1982). Some specifically cultural dimensions and implications of the process are treated in Archie Green, *Only a Miner: Studies in Recorded Coal-Mining Songs* (Urbana: University of Illinois Press, 1972).

16. John C. Campbell Folk School newsletter no. 18.

17. Morris, *Less Travelled Roads,* 79, quoting Ethel DeLong letter of January 1912.

18. *Mountain Life and Work* 4 (April 1928): 18.

19. *See* Jacquelyn D. Jones, *Soldiers of Light and Love: Northern Teachers and Southern Blacks, 1865–1873* (Chapel Hill: University of North Carolina Press, 1980) for an extended exploration of this point.

20. Blanche Wiesen Cook's "Female Support Networks and Political Activism: Lillian Wald, Crystal Eastman, Emma Goldman," in Nancy F. Cott and Elizabeth H. Pleck, eds., *A Heritage of Her Own* (New York: Simon and Schuster, 1979), 412–44, and Sara Evans's *Personal Politics: The Roots of Women's Liberation in the Civil Rights Movement and the New Left* (New York: Vintage Books, 1979) make some tentative but insightful explorations into the intimate interpersonal and sexual relationships between participants in social change movements at the turn of the century and in the 1960s.

21. John C. Campbell to John Glenn, May 8, 1913; Southern Historical Collection, University of North Carolina.

Teaching Traditional Fiddle in Shetland Isles Schools

BY PAMELA SWING

The Shetland Isles are a group of seventy islands that lie one hundred miles northeast of the Scottish mainland and approximately twice that distance west of Norway. Only twelve of the islands are currently inhabited. The islands are now the northernmost part of Great Britain, but prior to 1468 they belonged to Norway. Although this political shift took place over five hundred years ago, Shetlanders are proud of their Scandinavian heritage and the traces of it that have been retained. One example of this heritage is the Scandinavian influence on some of the oldest Shetland tunes. Another is in the fact that Shetlanders share with Scandinavians a strong preference for fiddle. Although the fiddle was introduced to Shetland from Scotland by the mid-1700s, the bagpipes, along with most other instruments, were not played in Shetland at all until the twentieth century. Thus for 150 years, the fiddle reigned supreme in the islands.

To have fiddle music formally taught in the schools represents a break from the traditional means of transmission, which was by ear and observation and very informal.

Tom Anderson giving a first lesson to a pupil in Islesburgh House, Lerwick. Photograph by Pamela Swing

A young boy (or much more rarely a young girl) would take an interest in fiddle music and try to pick up tunes on his own. He might get a few tips from older members of the family or neighboring relatives and friends who played. Or then again he might not. Fiddle teacher Tom Anderson described this family scene: "When my brother Jim was learning the fiddle, Bobby and I would sit and play tunes and deliberately not play the tune that Jim was working on. 'If you won't play that tune,' Jim would say, 'I'll just leave you.' 'Go away then,' Bobby would say, 'you're too young to learn—go to bed.' It might be 8:00 p.m. by then" (Swing, Journal, Dec. 16, 1984). Technique and tunes were not taught—learning was by imitation and by simply playing along. And even if a boy went to a fiddler to learn a specific tune, it would not be broken down for him phrase by phrase. Rather, he was expected to grasp the tune in its entirety. Traditional Shetland reels are short enough that such a feat of memory is possible. And the attitude towards note-for-note duplication was lax, so that both the experienced fiddler and novice were content so long as there was a rough idea of the tune. Certainly the large number of tune variants indicates this. When George Peterson gave Drew Robertson lessons on fiddle, he said Drew should not worry too much about individual notes—he hadn't when he learned the tunes. And George was sure the man he learned them from hadn't either. On the other hand, when Pat Shuldham Shaw collected tunes from Jena Stickle, Stickle insisted that the notes be just right. In this case, Stickle might have insisted because he was playing for a collector rather than another Shetlander.

The first big milestone for a fiddler was an invitation to play for a dance. This meant he had met some unspoken community standard. Tom Anderson remembers with pride being asked to play for his first wedding when he was thirteen. Although the fiddle was played in the home for the entertainment of family and visitors, or just to amuse the fiddler himself, the principal social outlet was to play for dancing: at weddings, over the festive season of Christmas and New Year's,[1] and on informal oc-

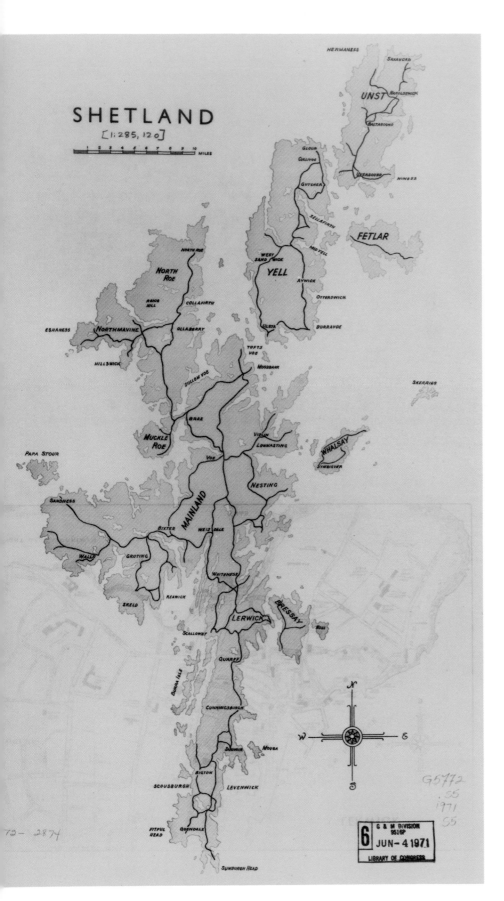

casions such as after an evening of communal spinning. This had a predictable influence on style—a strong rhythmic drive and volume were valued above subtleties of tone and polish. As long as the "lilt" and "quiff"* were there, actual notes could be sacrificed, lost in the digging in of the bow or the constant addition of open, ringing strings. The resulting sound was perhaps coarse, but it was vigorous and infectiously danceable.

The fiddle was held against the chest with the left wrist collapsed so that the fiddle rested against the arm. String crossings (going from one string to another) were achieved by shifting the fiddle from side to side rather than lifting the bow arm. This technique was made easier by using a flatter bridge than the standard violin bridge of today. The flatter bridge also made it simpler to play more than one string at a time. The fourth finger was not used, and fiddlers did not venture out of the first position. As with many European folk fiddling traditions, scordatura tunings (any that depart from the standard GDAE), were used in some regions for certain tunes. The most common were ADAE and AEAE. There was no fixed way to hold the bow; it was left to the individual fiddler to find a grip he liked. But the bow arm was generally stiff rather than loose. Bowing technique was far more complex than simple back and forth bowing, but the bow strokes took up only the upper-middle part of the bow. Playing reels for dancing did not require long, sustained tones, and vibrato was unknown. Specific bowing styles varied from island to island, and often between different communities on one island, as did tune repertoire. Presumably most fiddlers learned to play in the style of their home place, just as they learned their regional variant of the dialect. Some fiddlers acquired a reputation for being able to play tunes in different regional styles.

---

* Two Shetland musical terms that elude precise definition but which correspond to *swing* (as in jazz) and *oomph*.

Left: Map of the Shetland Islands, 1971. Geography and Map Division, Library of Congress

Right: George P. S. Peterson, formerly of Papa Sour, now a school teacher living in Brae, playing in the old style, with the fiddle pressed against his chest rather than under his chin. Photograph by Pamela Swing

The traditional method of learning and transmitting tunes that I have been describing is typical of a community where music is largely an aural phenomenon. Until this century, very few fiddlers could read music. Some of them learned sol-fa* at church for hymn singing, and attempted to write down tunes in this notation, but the most common means of transmission from one fiddler to another was by ear.

Starting at the turn of the century, music in Shetland became more diverse. It is a mistake to assume that the tradition was

static before the 1900s or that incorporating change, either in the form of new tunes or stylistic developments, was not the norm. Indeed, there is good evidence that Shetlanders favor ongoing adaptation over an adherence to old ways for the sake of keeping up traditions. Nevertheless, the pace of change accelerated after the turn of the century as technological advances such as the radio, engine-powered boats and ships, the telephone, and, later, airplanes forever lessened the isolation of the islands. Improved communication with the rest of the world had a strong effect on Shetlanders. John Harold Johnson described a period after World War I when people all over

* Using the syllables *do, re, me, fa, sol, la, ti* to sing the tones of the scale

Shetland rid themselves of old things in favor of new—carting furniture to throw over the banks into the sea, changing their style of dress, and as much as possible conforming to perceived standards of modernity. He views this period as one that broke with the past, leaving a sense of before and after, a gap that could never be bridged again.

The way this break manifested itself musically was severalfold. In a few short decades, major changes occurred that influenced every parameter of musical sound in Shetland. Community halls were built, so that dances were held in much larger spaces than croft houses and barns. New dances came in—waltzes, polkas, the Boston two-step, the eightsome reel, quadrilles, and more—that virtually replaced the Shetland reel. And along with the new dances came new tunes, supplemented by the wealth of new material suddenly available from the wireless and gramophone. Unaccompanied fiddle gave way to bands as guitar, piano, and the ever more popular accordion made their appearance. Today, the accordion, rather than the fiddle, is considered the best instrument for dancing, with its loud volume and ability to provide a rhythmic harmony to the melody. Small wonder amidst this wealth of change that traditional tunes and styles, and even the fiddles themselves, were quietly laid aside. Though Edmonston reported in 1809 that one in ten Shetlanders could play the instrument, there seem to be relatively few men of the post-World War II generation who can play at all. And those who did take up the fiddle learned Scottish or Irish tunes rather than Shetland tunes.

Eventually the pendulum started to swing in the other direction. As is usually the case when there has been such an irrevocable break with the past, there arose a romantic desire to collect and preserve traditions before they were lost forever. After World War II, in May 1945, the Shetland Folk Society was formed, and its members began collecting fiddle tunes. Society members included Tom Anderson, who was later to become a gifted and original teacher with a world-wide reputation. In the 1960s the Shetland Fiddlers' Society

was founded with the aim of playing traditional tunes. Without the work of the Folk Society and other collectors such as Tom Anderson and Pat Shuldham Shaw, there would have been few traditional Shetland fiddle tunes to teach. In Orkney, for example, only two traditional fiddle tunes survived.

In early 1973, Tom Anderson, who had recently retired from his lifelong career in the insurance business, saw an advertisement in the *Shetland Times* for a school violin teacher. When he went to apply for the job, the director of education, a Scotsman named John Spence, suggested he teach his own traditional music instead. The Education Committee was divided over this proposal but finally permitted him to try teaching on Saturday mornings, when the children were not in school.

No one was quite prepared for the response. As Tom described it to me: "The first Saturday I was snowballed. There were thirty-five children with their parents, all expecting tuition. I had to segregate them into various lots and send them home after five minutes and say, 'Look, I can't teach you all this in one go.'" After a few weeks the director of education decided he could teach on Fridays as well. "So," said Tom, "that's how it started" (Swing, Interview, Aug. 26, 1973, tape 73B2:15).

In order to understand what a radical change from past educational policies it was to offer official instruction in Shetland music, one must appreciate that up until very recently education in Shetland was geared first and foremost towards preparation for the nationwide Scottish exams. In order to ensure that Shetland students could compete, the curriculum had to conform closely to that found in the rest of Scotland. It was neither official policy nor, it was felt, in the best interest of the students, to offer courses in any aspect of Shetland culture or history since such material would never appear on an exam. Until the early 1970s, for example, the use of the local dialect was forbidden in the classroom,

Shetland Fiddlers Society, nicknamed "Da Forty Fiddlers," soon after it was formed in the 1960s. Tom Anderson, the charismatic teacher who spearheaded the movement to teach traditional fiddle playing in the schools, is standing slightly apart to the far right. The boy in the front row is Aly Bain, now a well-known fiddler in the folk group The Boys of the Lough. Courtesy of Pamela Swing, photographer unknown

and students who used it were punished. Even though it is now the official policy to encourage the use of dialect as a way to promote and preserve it, teachers still believe that learning "proper" English is more important for getting on in the outside world. Like many other things Shetland, local dialect has the stigma of being considered second-class to comparable items coming in from the outside.

By the early 1970s, certain vocationally oriented courses began to be offered in the schools that related directly to Shetland. These were courses in fishing, boatsmanship, and Fair Isle knitting. Fishing and knitting are two of the major traditional occupations in Shetland, though both have declined in recent years since the advent of the North Sea oil industries.

Oil was discovered off the coast of Shet-

land in 1971. By 1973, all of Shetland had realized that this discovery was going to have both immediate and long-range effects on many aspects of Shetland life. The general attitude was ambivalent: most Shetlanders wanted the economic advantages that oil would bring but were leery of the adverse effects on the culture and environment. The largest terminal in Great Britain was being planned at Sullum Voe, on the mainland of Shetland. Construction would require a massive influx of outside workers, who, along with their families, would have to be housed and somehow incorporated into the Shetland "way of life." When I first visited Shetland in 1973, the fear expressed by many was that they would be inundated by the incoming workers. It was generally felt that efforts must be made to preserve those aspects of the culture that were felt to

The original 1984 class of fiddle students at the Uyeasound School on the island of Unst. Steven Spence, who has since graduated from school and developed his own individual style of play, is the last one in the front row on the right. Photograph by Pamela Swing

be of value. Disagreements arose as to what those aspects specifically were, but most agreed that measures had to be taken.

So it was in this climate that Tom Anderson's application for the position of violin instructor was met with the counter suggestion that he teach "his own traditional music." The time was ripe for such a formal gesture. The Education Committee may have been ambivalent, but the overwhelming response from the children and their parents, and the continuing success of the program, shows that the director of education had correctly gauged the interest of the community.

The success of the pilot program did not go unnoticed in the rest of Shetland. First the headmaster of the Baltasound School on the island of Unst and then a Shetland Islands council member for the island of Yell petitioned for extension to the North Isles. In the spring of 1974, Tom Anderson began weekly trips to both islands. It just so happened that I was spending that year in Shetland studying traditional fiddle with him myself. I became his assistant, a position that was later officially sanctioned by the Education Committee, and together that year we started fiddle classes in five schools: Uyeasound and Baltasound schools on Unst, and Cullivoe, Mid Yell, and Burravoe schools on Yell. By the end of the year we were teaching eighty-four pupils a week.

Participation in the program was voluntary. Teachers informed their classes that fiddle lessons were available, and anyone over the age of seven was eligible to take them. Once again the response was overwhelming. The entire upper primary school of Uyeasound wanted to take fiddle lessons. Steven Spence, a Uyeasound pupil, became so enthusiastic that he practiced or listened to records for hours every night and insisted on sleeping with his fiddle. A girl in the Mid Yell school who fell just short of the age cutoff was so bitterly disappointed that they waived the age requirement for her. She later, incidentally, became a teacher of Shetland fiddle herself.

It was up to the students to obtain instruments. The former popularity of fiddle music in Shetland meant there were instruments around, though usually only full-sized and often in poor condition. The first few weeks that a program began at a new school were invariably spent looking over the wide variety of instruments (I remember one came as an assortment of pieces jumbled together in a plastic bag). We would take carloads of them back to Lerwick to be repaired by Alex Leask, a local self-taught fiddle maker. Fiddles could also be purchased in Lerwick—usually inexpensive Chinese models in smaller sizes that served their purpose as learning instruments but sounded like the mass-produced instruments they were.

At first, students were taught in classes of four or five at a time, grouped according to age initially and later by level of proficiency. As the program progressed, instruction came to be on an individual basis or at most in groups of two. Our teaching method was experimental at first and improved as we went along. We started everyone off with the basics of holding the instrument (under the chin, not against the chest as the old fiddlers did) and holding the bow, and then taught simple bowing and fingering exercises. Tom's strategy with beginning students was to have them play simple tunes as soon as possible, so that they felt as if they were making music. Even the "Grand Old Duck of York," with a simple piano back up, was sufficient to ignite the spark and turn the desire to play fiddle into a reality. Tom would emphasize over and over again in early lessons that playing fiddle was fun. And in spite of their initial faulty intonation and awkward bowing, most students gained a strong sense of the joy of music-making in remarkably short order.

As Tom became a more experienced teacher, he developed a rough guide to the stages of progress. "The plodders go one step at a time. Some jump a few steps, take on more than one tune, or start experimenting, which I never condemn. One out of ten makes a gigantic leap. But I must judge each on their own" (Swing, Journal, Dec. 16, 1984). Teaching was tailored to the individual student. Tom is very sensitive to the attention span of youngsters and has an uncanny sense of how to present something so that it appeals to a particular child.

Certain tunes became heuristic devices for introducing new techniques, and were used in place of exercises. After the initial stage of learning to hold the instrument and playing a first tune such as "Baa Baa Black Sheep," a student is given his first real Shetland tune, "Bonnie Tammie Scollay." Shetland bowings are introduced with "Da Broon Coo," a Shetland version of "Mrs. MacLeod." A waltz is useful for getting pupils to use the full length of the bow. The Shetland reel "Donald Blue" is good for teaching the Shetland bowing "one down and three up," [2] and "Da Lerwick Lasses" is ideal for showing the "stop-go" effect of rhythm. "Da Day Dawn" and "Christmas Day ida Moarning" are introduced to get them used to old melodies. Once they have mastered bowings, Tom goes on to other technical and stylistic refinements:

I'm never really finished: there's accents, ringing strings, keeping the bite in their playing. Then there's positions and other tricks for slow airs, flat keys, use of the fourth finger, and vibrato. When they have the Shetland repertoire, both traditional and contemporary, under their belt, then I introduce them to Scottish strathspeys and some Scandinavian tunes (Swing, Journal, Dec. 16, 1984).

Scottish dance band tunes, Irish tunes, and American country and western music are never taught in Tom's lessons. The other instructors are less adamant about maintaining a distinction, although I would be surprised to learn that a country and western tune was being taught.

In 1976, Tom and I began the task of formalizing the teaching repertoire by producing a small book of fiddle tunes called *Haand Me Doon da Fiddle*. We included the story behind each tune written in the dialect, and asked the fiddle students to do illustrations. The book was published in 1978, and was followed by *Ringing Strings* in 1983 and *Gie Us an A* in 1987. *Haand Me Doon da Fiddle* consists of traditional tunes, with a sprinkling of contemporary ones mostly by Tom Anderson. The other two books have a much larger proportion of Tom Anderson compositions. Since the 1900s, tunes composed by specific Shetlanders have been identified as such. There have been many composers in Shetland, and Gideon Stove, Ronnie Cooper, and Tom Anderson are the best known. Although all their tunes, especially Ronnie Cooper's, are played by Shetland dance bands, Tom Anderson has used primarily his own tunes in the classroom.

From the start, Tom taught pupils how to read music at the same time they learned to play fiddle. He considers the ability essential for fiddlers these days. Teaching tunes from music represented a radical departure from the past, when music was transmitted by ear. Admittedly, by the 1970s, picking up tunes from music was no longer a startling innovation. A number of musicians, including Tom, had taught themselves to read music. But, in general, reading music was seen as a means of gaining access to non-Shetland tunes. Tom found nothing incongruous about teaching traditional Shetland tunes from music. This attitude differs markedly from that in Norway, which has also experienced a renaissance of its traditional fiddle music. In Norway, oral transmission is seen as an integral part of the tradition, although printed resources are also consulted. But according to Jan Petter Blom, a Norwegian ethnomusicologist, there is a general sense that picking up a tune by ear allows transmission of stylistic aspects that are difficult if not impossible to convey through the printed music. In Shetland, however, the attitude over the last fifty years or so has been that oral transmission is limiting, since it restricts the fiddler to the tunes he can hear. A number of fiddlers I approached said, "What can I show you? I can't even read music." The statement implies that music they learned by ear, that is, tunes played locally, is of less value than music that has been written down, that is, non-Shetland tunes. Since music transmitted by ear has been stigmatized in this way, teaching Shetland music from the printed page can be

seen as a way of giving it a higher status and putting it more on a level with other printed music. It is also generally felt in Shetland that teaching orally limits what actually is taught. As Tom says:

I saw it with John Henderson learning from his father, Willie Barclay Henderson—he imitated completely. Today you've got to analyze it. I fail to see that you can do it any other way today and teach the technique of the fiddle. You would leave your pupil with complete oral teaching without any idea of what he was doing. And it would take longer (Swing, Interview, Oct. 11, 1976, tape 76D1:4).

None of the instructors currently teaching fiddle in the schools saw picking up tunes by ear as a positive skill that could be fostered and developed, though all of them were aware that some pupils cheated and were only pretending to read music after having memorized their tunes by ear. Margaret Robertson was particularly adept at this, and had to do some quick remedial work before she could be hired as a fiddle instructor herself. But as a result of her own experience, she is adamant that her pupils learn to read.

For Tom, the opportunity to teach fiddle in a school represented a lot more than just the chance to perpetuate the traditional tunes, though that was a crucial element. It was also the opportunity to produce expert fiddlers. So technique quickly became an integral part of fiddle lessons. As Tom said:

In my opinion, a lot of these so-called "good" fiddlers for dancing had good rhythm but no technique at all. They just sawed it out. If an instrument is worth playing, it's worth playing well. . . . It requires a certain amount of practice and technique. . . . Look at the quality of young fiddlers today—they're playing traditional tunes in an authentic traditional style. But look at the tone they use, and the sound they are getting. Older fiddlers didn't get that tone. . . . It's better for the fiddle—it's giving of its best (Swing, Interview, Oct. 11, 1976, tape 76Dl:1).

Restricting the current batch of young fiddlers to the level of proficiency of the old

Shetland fiddlers is also perceived by Tom (and most other Shetlanders) as a limitation. Holding the fiddle under the chin rather than against the chest, for example, permits the use of higher positions and vibrato. And holding the bow at the frog instead of "half mast" allows for longer and smoother bows, "dancing" bow (spiccato), and other bowing techniques. But something is lost as well—the very roughness of the old way of playing could, as it is in Norway, have been seen as an important characteristic of the style. But in Tom's view (and that of other Shetlanders), these changes are improvements. Thus Tom's approach to teaching the tradition is to leave the notes the same but "improve" the style in which the tune is played. As he puts it:

The fiddle is a tool, and like any tool it can be misused. A good carpenter doesn't misuse his saw, his chisel. Even the old men knew that. So why not the fiddle. I contend that technique should be taught. It may make the old tunes sound smoother, better tone, lose the edge, lose the roughness. It's the difference between a rough box being made by an amateur and a cabinet being made by a cabinet maker (Swing, Interview, Oct. 11, 1976, tape 76D1:7).

This whole issue of teaching fiddle technique and improving the style impinges on another issue, namely that the teaching program is consciously aimed at turning out concert performers rather than dance musicians. This is not to say that Tom does not emphasize the fact that Shetland music was once largely a dance music tradition. In fact he goes to great lengths to impart stylistic features that he feels characterize dancing fiddlers' styles of playing. But the major traditional dance of Shetland was the Shetland Reel, and it is rarely danced today. Even if the school program were to include the teaching of dance, it is highly unrealistic to assume Shetlanders would want to return to dances of yore, especially in view of the fact that the Shetland Reel, and only the Shetland Reel, was danced for twelve hours at a stretch. But rather than teach other dance tunes, such as the ones heard in Shetland dance halls today, Tom stresses technical proficiency so as to raise the status of Shetland traditional tunes to that of music listened to carefully as well as danced to. By so doing, he creates a forum for a number of unique Shetland tunes that were never danced to and that would otherwise by now have completely disappeared. These are the so-called "descriptive tunes," [3] such as the "Full Rigged Ship," wedding tunes, and various other tunes that defy categorization. As Tom puts it:

There are certain tunes in Shetland which are classical, as in any folk music. What is classical? That which is put in a class. . . . Shetland has a right to its own classical music. It should come near to its natural sounds, that is, the sounds of nature. . . . What we've got here are these beautiful old melodies. Take "Da Day Dawn"—look at the cadences. You can actually hear the sun starting to come up, probably a fine morning, with a gentle breeze, and probably the sea at the banks, going "sh-sh-sh" [sings]. You can hear the flow of the sea in that. Now if that's not a classic, nothing is (Swing, Interview, Oct. 11, 1976, tape 76D1:7).

What Tom has done here is to create a new tradition from the ashes of the old. "Da Day Dawn," for example, survived into modern times only in written form. The other so-called descriptive tunes came mostly from two fiddlers, Peter Fraser of the Westside and Jena Stickle from Unst, both of whom were the last surviving players of their regional tradition. Tom's interpretation of how those tunes were once played has given a new life to them, one that may have been implicit in them before but was probably never described in quite his way. Tom has a gift for describing the story behind a tune, thus imparting to the students a deep sense of what the music is about and how it should be played. Some of the stories have been handed down in tradition; others, like "Da Day Dawn," are his own creations. This story-telling ability is one of the reasons he is such a great teacher—and it is easy to see why Tom prefers the stage to the dance hall. The stories provide a natural presentational format for the tunes, which would be lost completely in a dance set. The stage also provides a forum for putting the tunes in historical context. Ultimately, what Tom is trying to impart to his pupils through the fiddle-teaching program is a sense of their own heritage.

Now it is tempting to end with that. But of course the story does not end there because it is the students themselves who make what they will of their fiddle lessons. So I will end with a brief look at some of the results of the program. There are many encouraging things that have happened. Over seven hundred children have received fiddle lessons. Most are competent musicians, and quite a few have become excellent fiddlers who can be heard in concerts, broadcasts, and on recordings. Some have tried their hand at composing; others have turned to fiddle making. In 1981, the Shetland Folk Society instituted a "Young Fiddler of the Year" competition with the aim of promoting youthful interest in fiddle music. In 1983, some of Tom Anderson's students formed a group called Shetland Young Heritage, which has performed throughout Shetland, in Norway, Scotland, and before royalty in England. Two former pupils, Trevor Hunter and Margaret Robertson, are now instructors themselves. Another pupil, Catriona MacDonald, is currently studying music at university with the aim of coming back to teach. And there are several other potential teachers currently acting as assistants. Throughout Shetland there has been a renaissance of music-making as new musicians have joined the ranks. Often, the presence of one or more fiddle students in a family has en-

Shetland's Young Heritage in Concert at Cunningsburgh Hall, on the Mainland of Shetland. Tom Anderson is seated to the far right and Catriona MacDonald is in the back row, far left. Photograph by Pamela Swing

Trevor Hunter teaching a pupil in the Uyeasound School. Trevor teaches fiddle full-time and is also the current leader of the Shetland Fiddlers Society and the recently formed Junior Shetland Fiddlers. Photograph by Pamela Swing

couraged a father, mother, or other live-in relative to take up the fiddle or some other instrument again. The teaching program is generally credited with putting fiddle playing back on its feet in Shetland.

But what about the aim of passing on the tradition? This is more problematic. The tradition of Shetland music as the primary form of music in Shetland and as an integral part of most social occasions has not been passed on. Shetland traditional tunes are but a small part of the diversity of musics available to Shetlanders today. In some ways I find it remarkable that Shetland children want to learn traditional fiddle at all, given the strong youthful interest in rock, pop, and disco. And some fiddle students spoke of being teased on the playground for learning to play fiddle. Nevertheless the Young Heritage group has received wide recognition—thanks in large measure to Tom Anderson's worldwide reputation and ability to promote. The members of the group enjoy the prestige, and the chance to join is a powerful incentive for struggling fiddle students. A tradition of presenting Shetland traditional tunes in concert is well on its way to being established. So is it safe

to say that at least the tunes have been saved?

The answer is complicated. For one thing, the wealth of regional variants in both tunes and styles of playing has fallen by the wayside. Although Tom does make a token effort to teach more than one regional style, the general effect is a pan-Shetland style, and only one version of each tune is ever taught. Furthermore, teaching from music almost unavoidably leads to the desire to get the notes exactly as written. And despite the fact that there are still a few old traditional fiddlers around, none of the students go to visit them to learn their versions of tunes. In some sense what is being taught in the schools is the Tom Anderson tradition of fiddle playing. He is a very charismatic teacher and the loyalty he inspires can be fierce. One student, when I asked what she liked best about fiddle lessons, replied:

Just the fact that Tom Anderson was my hero. I thought of him as famous. And the fact that it was a traditional instrument, gone through the past, and I'm sitting there and able to play myself. The thrill of being able to play, and to think, my granddad

Willie Johnson (guitar), Davy Tulloch (fiddle), and John Dalziel (piano), performing in a Lerwick pub. Tulloch now resides in Scotland. He has produced an album and is working on another. Photograph by Pamela Swing

played too. You'd learn a tune, and rush home and play it. It was a gift, something to be proud of. I couldn't wait to get to me fiddle lessons (Swing, Interview, 1984).

But most students I talked to did not take up the fiddle because they wanted to learn Shetland traditional tunes. They did it because their friends, or older sister or brother, were doing it, or because their parents wanted them to. A lot of them put up with the old tunes because "Tammie," as Tom is called in Shetland, insists on it. Here's one student's frank assessment of the situation:

Folk don't want to hear the old tunes. We just play them to please Tammie. We get a better response in Scotland and Norway, whereas they yawned at the Hardanger fiddle music in Norway. Better to let other folk outside Shetland learn the tunes, here they're fed up with it. I played "Da Full Rigged Ship" once and a man asked, "Has du played a fiddle afore?" I was really in-sulted. We've played them so much in Young Heritage that me and ——— just cringe. Tammie doesn't understand how fed up we are (Swing, Interview, 1984).

At home they play a variety of other tunes, go to disco dances, and even experiment with changing the way they play the traditional tunes. Even the young lady just quoted on how much she loved fiddle lessons does not hesitate to play the tunes her own way. She is just very careful to make sure "Tammie" does not find out. In a sense, her explorations are more in keeping with the tradition of picking up the gist of a tune and then making it your own. Some students have graduated from school and gone off in their own directions, such as Davy Tulloch, Debbie Scott, and Steve Spence, who all have strong individual styles and eclectic musical tastes. For the majority of students, it remains to be seen what they will make of their fiddle lessons.

NOTES

1. In Shetland one says "New Year's" but not "New Year's Eve." Christmas there used to be known as "Yule," and New Year's Eve blended into a festive season that stretched out for several weeks. During this time, people put their work aside and visited each other for whole nights of music-making, dancing, and general merriment. Christmas was not celebrated as it is in America today. There was no Christmas tree, and only small gifts were given to the children. There would be a special meal during the day, but the main emphasis was on the celebration at night.

2. "One down and three up" refers to a bowing pattern in which one eighth note is on the down stroke of the bow, and the three following eighth notes are slurred together on the up stroke. This pattern can either happen just once or be repeated several times. The single eighth note can either be on the strong beat or the off beat of the measure. When it is on the off beat, the music is syncopated. The off-beat "one down and three up" bowing is one of the most characteristic Shetland bowings and is much of what gives Shetland music a distinctive flavor. Scottish fiddlers, for example, would never use that particular bowing.

3. Tom Anderson has created the label "descriptive tunes" for tunes in which melodic effects seem to "describe" something. Thus "Da Full Rigged Ship" depicts a three-masted schooner at sea. As Tom puts it in *Ringing Strings*, "It describes the motion of a full-rigged ship with a nice sailing wind. The changes in tempo try to describe where the ship and sea play a little game" (page 58).

REFERENCES

Anderson, Tom. *Gie's an A.* Lerwick: Shetland Musical Heritage Trust, 1986.

————. *Ringing Strings: Traditional Shetland Music and Dance.* Lerwick: The Shetland Times, Ltd., 1983.

Anderson, Tom, and Tom Georgeson. *Da Mirrie Dancers: A Book of Shetland Fiddle Tunes.* 2d ed. Lerwick: Shetland Folk Society, 1985.

Anderson, Tom, and Pam Swing. *Haand Me Doon da Fiddle.* Stirling: Department of Continuing Education, University of Stirling, 1979.

Cooke, Peter. *The Fiddle Tradition of the Shetland Isles.* Cambridge: Cambridge University Press, 1987.

Edmondston, Arthur M.D. *A View of the Ancient and Present State of the Zetland Islands.* 2 vols. Edinburgh: James Ballantyne and Co., 1809.

Flett, J.F., and T.M. *Traditional Dancing in Scotland.* London: Routledge and Kegan Paul, 1964.

DISCOGRAPHY

Aly Bain. Whirlie 001.139, 1984.

Curlew: Fiddle Music from Shetland and Beyond. Topic 12TS435, 1985.

Eftir da Humin, Vols. 1 and 2. Shetland Folk Society. Thule Records TAP 4000 and 4006.

Haand Me Doon da Fiddle. Stirling: Department of Continuing Education, University of Stirling, 1978.

Me and My Shadows: Steven Spence. Viking Vision ZEO12, 1983.

Da Merrie Boys: Shetland Fiddle Tunes Collected by Pat Shaw. Folktracks FSD-60–068, 1978.

Scottish Tradition 4: Shetland Fiddle Music. School of Scottish Studies, University of Edinburgh. Tangent TNGM 117, 1973.

Shetland Fiddlers. Leader LED 2052, 1973.

Shetland Folk Fiddling, Vol. 2. Topic 12TS379, 1978.

The Silver Bow: Shetland Folk Fiddling, Vol. 1. Topic 12TS281, 1976.

Willie Hunter 1982: Fiddle Music from Shetland and Scotland. Celtic Music CM 010, 1982.

A Fraktur Primer

BY DON YODER

Haus-Segen (house blessing). Woodcut with letterpress, watercolor and gouache; 39.5 × 32 cm (sheet). Imprint: Allentaun, [Pennsylvania], Gedruckt und zu haben bei Graeter und Blumer (LC-USZ62-93914; LC-USZC4-1214)

In 1923, Mrs. Anna Louise Jenks, a government clerk from Landover, Prince Georges County, Maryland, gave six frakturs to the Library of Congress. The gift included one birth certificate decorated by Johannes Schopp, two hymns of Johann Franck, lettered by Henrich Rassmann, and two manuscript epistles of St. Paul and one Wisdom of Sirach verse, decorated in Lancaster County, Pennsylvania. Several dozen more such frakturs were included in a collection of Pennsylvania German and other American primitive prints and drawings, acquired from Karl Goedecke of Hazleton, Pennsylvania, in 1943.

In the years following the Jenks gift, the Library has acquired many broadsides printed in German, with woodcut illustrations of the Ages of Man, Adam and Eve, selfishness vs. generosity, letters from God, and folksongs. The collection of illuminated manuscripts includes vows of celibacy at the Ephrata Cloister in Lancaster County and the popular birth and baptismal certificates "finished" by Friederich Krebs, with wide-eyed parrots and swelling turnip-shaped hearts.

The manuscripts and prints reflect the religious interest of the Lutheran, Reformed, Schwenkfelder, and Anabaptist communities. They demonstrate a skill in calligraphy and an appreciation of hymnody, poetry, and humor. This documentation from Pennsylvania Dutch communities reveals a good deal about their religious beliefs, habits, and decorative arts from the mid-1700s to the early 1900s.

In 1988, the American Folklife Center published a guide to the fraktur collections in the Library of Congress, Pennsylvania German Fraktur and Printed Broadsides. The following introduction to the subject is from that guide.

Fraktur is a phenomenon in the world of American folk art rooted in the Pennsylvania Dutch (Pennsylvania German) culture. The word *fraktur*, when used for a type of art, is an Americanism. In German, the word means either a particular typeface used by printers or letters made into designs. Based on the Latin *fractura*, a "breaking apart," fraktur suggests that the letters are broken apart and reassembled into designs.

In the world of American collecting and connoisseurship, fraktur as a genre of folk art refers to a folk art drawn, penned, and painted on paper, i.e., *manuscript* folk art. Fraktur centers around a text (usually religious), that is decorated to varying degrees with symbolic designs. In Europe, and also in Pennsylvania, the earlier word for such pieces of art was *Frakturschriften* or "Fraktur Writings." (This term is reflected in the title of the book that I consider to be the best historical introduction to the subject, Donald A. Shelley's 1961 *The Franktur-Writings or Illuminated Manuscripts of the Pennsylvania Germans*.) *Fraktur* then is short for *Frakturschriften*.

To call fraktur an American phenomenon, one must explain that while its earlier roots lie in the European parent cultures of our Pennsylvania Dutch world, in the arts of Switzerland and the Rhine Valley, it blossomed and developed in new directions in America. Here it came to form an even more basic part of everyday culture. Fraktur documents did exist in Europe, but the

Mein Gott und Vater segne mich;
Der Sohn erhalte gnädiglich
Was er mir hat gegeben.
Der Geist erleuchte Tag und Nacht
Sein Antlitz über mich mit Macht
Und schütze mir mein Leben.
Nur dieses wünsch' ich für und für,
Der Segen Gottes sei mit mir.

Laß Herr dein'n Segen auf mir ruhn,
Mich deine Wege wallen
Und lehre du mich selber thun
Nach deinem Wohlgefallen.
Nimm meines Lebens gnädig wahr;
Auf dich hofft meine Seele;
Sei mir ein Retter in Gefahr
Ein Vater wann ich fehle.

Haus-Segen.

In den drei allerhöchsten Namen,
Vater, Sohn und Heil'ger Geist,
Die das Chor der Engel preißt,
Gesundheit, Ruh' und Segen, Amen.

Gott des Vaters Schöpfers Hand
Segne dieses Haus und Land,
Daß das Futter und die Saaten
Immer mögen wohlgerathen;
Daß der Viehstand wohl gedeihe,
Und sich seines Segens freue.
Daß seine väterliche Güte
Haus und Hof und Stall und Scheuer
Vor Unglück und besonders Feuer.
Immer gnädiglich behüte.

Auch geb er, daß auf jeder Wange
Die edele Gesundheit prange
Und zur Vollendung unsrer Werke.
Geb' er den Gliedern Kraft und Stärke.
Er wende von uns in Gnaden
Hagel- und Gewitter-Schaden.
Auch wolle er die zarten Blüthen
Vor später Kält' und Frost behüten.

Mögen des Erlösers Werke
Ihre Kraft und ihre Stärke
Stets an diesem Haus beweisen;
Daß jedes d'rinn nach Tugend strebe
Und friedlich mit dem andern lebe
Und guten Wandels sich befleiße;
Daß Schand' und Laster insgemein
Entfernt von diesem Hause sein.

Der heil'ge Geist kehr hier auch ein
Und laß' es seine Wohnung sein,
Heil'ge unser Thun und Lassen,
Aus- und Ein-Gang gleichermaßen;
Heil'ge uns zum sel'gen Sterben
Und mach' uns zu Himmels-Erben. — Amen.

Allentaun, [Penns.]
Gedruckt und zu haben bei Gräter und Blumer.

Haus-Segen (house blessing). Woodcut with letterpress and watercolor, on wove paper; 40.5 × 33.5 cm (sheet). Signed: G. Miesse SC. (Gabriel Miesse, 1807–1886)

environment. In this cultural blend, fraktur became the principal genre of art available for viewing by the Pennsylvania Dutch. True, a few well-to-do farmers and townsfolk had their portraits painted, and framed prints are mentioned occasionally in inventories of household goods. Painted furniture, tavern signs, and tombstones were also at that time to be looked at as art. But for a century, from the mid-eighteenth to mid-nineteenth century, fraktur remained the form of art closest to the Pennsylvania Dutchman and his family.

What was the subject matter of fraktur? Fraktur was a private art, dealing with the role of the individual in Pennsylvania Dutch society. Anthropologists speak of the "rites of passage," the appropriate rituals that attend those life crises when the individual passes from one group in his close-knit society to another. These folk graduation ceremonies, so to speak, involved birth and baptism; puberty, schooling, and confirmation; courtship and marriage; and death and funeral rites.

Most individuals in Pennsylvania Dutch society passed through all these sacred portals. A few individuals escaped marriage, remaining through life in the role of maiden aunt or bachelor uncle, important parts of the extended family in the massive Pennsylvania farmhouses.

The special fraktur documents associated with each of the above rites of passage are: (1) the Birth and Baptismal Certificate (*Taufschein*), (2) the Calligraphic Model, Reward of Merit, or Lastday Gift of Teacher to Student (*Vorschrift*), (3) the Confirmation Certificate (*Confirmationsschein*), (4) the Wedding Certificate (*Trauschein*), and (5) the Memorial (*Denkmal*). Of these the *taufschein* and the *vorschrift* form the vast bulk of fraktur documentation. Wedding and death certificates are relatively rare. For weddings there was another form of art available: the wedding plate with its humorous inscription. For death and burial there was the engraved tombstone.

Pennsylvania Dutchman's ancestors there were exposed to a much wider range of artistic expression than their descendants in eighteenth- and nineteenth-century America. In Pennsylvania during the early settlement era, fraktur art flowered, at least in part, to fill an artistic vacuum that existed in the everyday world of the Pennsylvania Dutch farmer.

Fraktur flowered in the colonial era when those forefathers of the Pennsylvania Dutch (German-speaking emigrants from the Rhineland and Switzerland) settled together in Pennsylvania over an area the size of Switzerland. Cutting their cultural ties with Europe, they developed an original and creative culture on American soil by applying their traditional crafts and craftsmanship to the problems of the American

A few other genres of fraktur exist, for example the Valentine or True Lover's Knot (forms shared with Anglo-American cultures) and the House Blessing (*Haussegen*). In addition there are also found fraktur ballads and hymns, fraktur Bible records, fraktur mottoes, fraktur alphabet books, and fraktur title or inscription pages of gift books, Bibles, testaments, church records, and manuscript music books used in singing schools. All of these examples can be considered fraktur art since they combine the two necessary elements—a text done in fraktur lettering and designs surrounding or embellishing the text. Occasionally one also finds watercolor or pen and ink pictures that some scholars subsume under the fraktur rubric even though the picture itself dominates the piece and there is very little lettering. These were usually called by their makers not *Frakturschriften* but *Bilder*—"pictures."

Who produced fraktur? While it used to be popular to suppose that "folk" art was produced indiscriminately by everyone in a "folk" culture, from toddler to nonagenarian, reason and research finally demonstrated that, in traditional societies like that of rural Pennsylvania, the "folk" art was produced by specialists. The average Pennsylvania Dutchman did not produce his fraktur baptismal certificate any more than he constructed his house single-handed, or built his very own Conestoga wagon. Even in its pioneer stages of settlement, every rural community was indeed a community of craftsmen and clients, of producers and consumers, of builders and buyers.

In these country communities, and eventually in the small towns that grew up as trade centers, the individuals whom we dignify with the name "fraktur artists" did indeed produce art for their communities; but their production was a sideline to their major occupations. They were not studio artists producing public art for a wealthy clientele, but individuals who, in addition to their major occupation, produced private art for private individuals with whom they came in contact in church and school.

The great majority of the artists who produced the thousands of pieces that we admire today were either ministers in the Lutheran and Reformed churches—the majority religions of the Pennsylvania Dutch—or schoolmasters in the parochial schools run by these churches or by the sectarian groups such as the Mennonites, Brethren, and Schwenkfelders. The Moravians produced relatively little fraktur. (This is probably because Moravianism produced a much broader spectrum of elite art like portraiture and religious paintings, which were part of every Moravian's visual world.) In the exciting detective work to identify the now unknown frakturists, the great majority are turning out to be country schoolmasters.

What was the function of fraktur art? In any society, from the primitive to the complex, art has multiple functions. Taking the functionalist view of culture, art is only one integral part of a larger cultural whole in which all parts of the culture interact with each other. But an analysis of the art produced by a culture can lead us to an understanding of the meanings, the world-view, the value systems of the society that produced the culture. So the first function of fraktur art is the recording of events in an individual's life, as he or she moves through the rites of passage from one social group into the next. These transitions were essentially the four rites of passage introduced earlier: (1) from nameless and unbaptized infant to named and baptized person; (2) from baptized to confirmed membership in the church; (3) from teenage, unmarried, and dependent status to adult, married, and independent status in a new household; and (4) from (as Swiss folklife scholar Richard Weiss put it) the community of the living to the community of the dead. Thus regarded, the documents that recorded these changes of state and status were intensely personal. They were made for and meant for individuals, who

Birth certificate for Jacob Meily, b. 1774. Pen and brown ink over pencil, with watercolor, on laid paper; 20.5 × 25.5 cm (sheet). Artist unknown

treasured them through life. Hence most fraktur art is an art for the individual, that is, a private rather than a public art.

The individual to whom the piece belonged and for whom it was made could take comfort throughout life from reading "his" or "her" texts, remembering the gift and the maker, and receiving spiritual encouragement from the words. The texts themselves were part of the Pennsylvania Dutchman's broad repertoire of devotional reading from Bible, hymnal, and prayerbook.

Fraktur was a permitted form of art in cultures that frowned upon public art and public display. The sectarian groups in the Pennsylvania Dutch world—Mennonites, Brethren, Schwenkfelders, Amish, and oth-

ers—took a negative, essentially puritan view of art. Public art, art for display, was forbidden. Therefore fraktur—private, unobtrusive, and essentially Protestant in its emphasis on religious texts—became a permitted form of art in all the Pennsylvania Dutch groups.

Fraktur both delights the eye and refreshes the spirit. The bright colors, the ingenious combination of text, picture, and overall design, and the curious and now archaic folk symbols are a visual delight whether or not we understand the symbolic and cultural implications behind them. For example, mermaids were often put on baptismal certificates, representing the water spirits in lakes and springs. In Germanic mythology these were believed to deliver newborn babies to the midwives, who then took them back to the waiting mothers. At least this was the story as told to curious Dutch children, just as Anglo-Americans use the stork as symbol of birth. And who can resist those portly Dutch angels blowing trumpets of joy and all those fiddling and dancing figures on a baptismal certificate? They go far to convince us that in the old days the birth and baptism of a child was a real occasion of joy in family and community. There was often, in fact, a Pennsylvania Dutch baptismal party at which the birth and the newly named child were celebrated.

A study of fraktur art enables us to begin to understand the complex belief systems of the Pennsylvania Dutch culture. As most of the texts are religious, they are often the key to central beliefs, clues both to religious faith and the way in which this faith translated into behavior.

How was fraktur displayed in the traditional Pennsylvania Dutch home? Actually, most of it wasn't. Today we frame and display fraktur pieces on our walls, using them as decoration, museums have "fraktur rooms," but our Pennsylvania Dutch forefathers usually kept their highly individual fraktur pieces, fortunately for us, away from the light, in Bibles or other large books, pasted onto the inside lids of blanket chests, or rolled up in bureau drawers. I

Birth and baptismal certificate for Catharina Heilman, b. 1777. Woodcut with letterpress, watercolor, and pen and ink, on laid paper; 33 × 41 cm (sheet). Artist unknown (LC-USZ62-93917; LC-USZC4-1216)

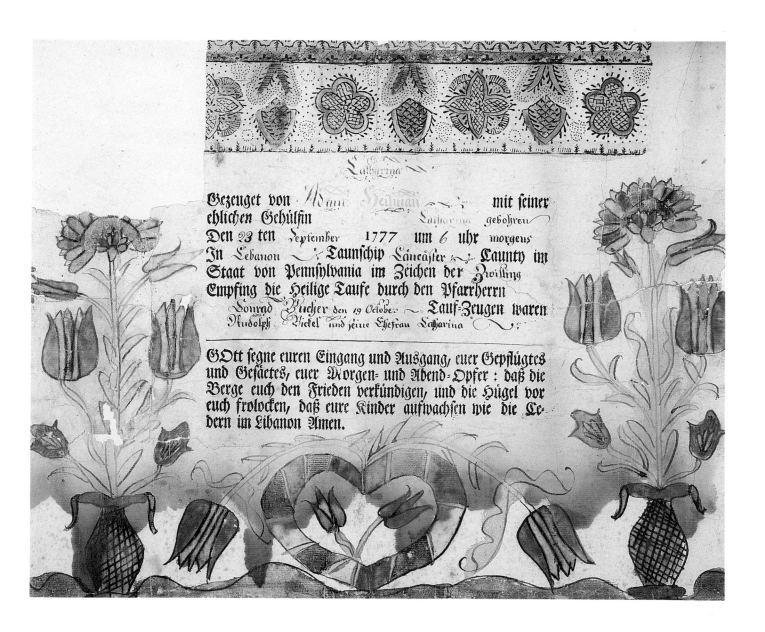

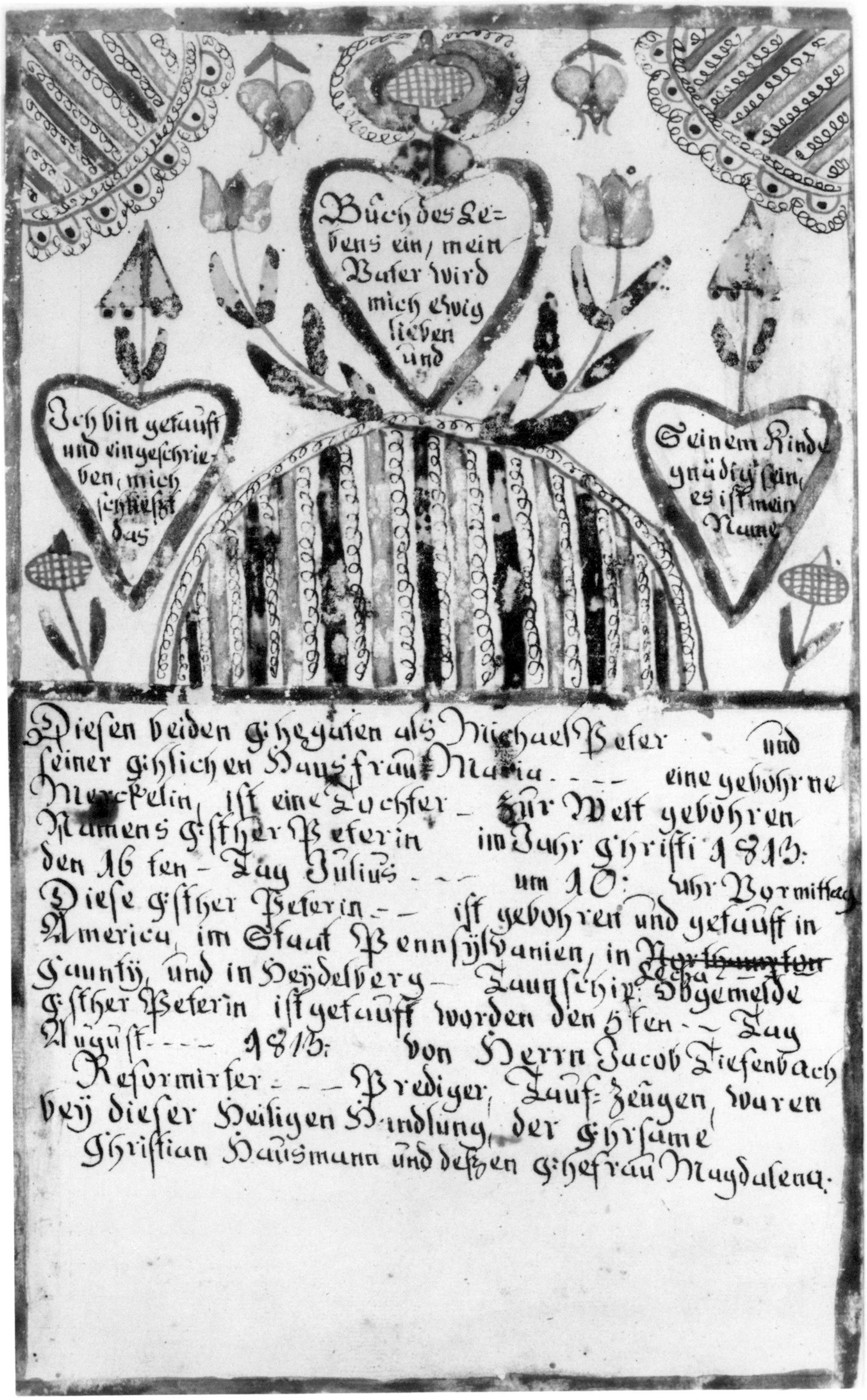

will never forget that thrilling moment in my own life when one of my favorite Dutch aunts opened her bureau drawer and presented me with a roll of all my family's fraktur documents from the 1780s to the 1860s. I do not, however, keep them in my bureau drawer. Yielding to current custom, I had most of them framed, and I occasionally display them on walls, walls that do not receive direct sunlight.

Although they often bear some resemblance to fraktur, prints made by the Penn-

sylvania Dutch were something else. They were often framed and put on the walls of homes and taverns, where they functioned as visual art with all its nuances. The up-country and city presses of the Pennsylvania Dutch culture were busy in the late eighteenth and first half of the nineteenth century producing broadsides and prints.

These two, broadsides and prints, are closely related. A broadside is by definition a sheet of paper printed on one side. This definition could include the print as well, except that we usually divide them by insisting that a broadside features a text and a print features a picture. Broadsides were ephemeral, their purpose was to note passing events. They began, in fact, as vehicles for spreading news, and long continued as an adjunct to the newspaper. For example, tragedies, local as well as national, were recorded on broadsides, often in the form of a lugubrious ballad that was sung on the streets and in the marketplace, wherever people gathered. People learned the tune from hearing a street singer perform the many verses of the song, and paid the singer a penny or two for the broadside to remember the words.

There was a significant transfer from the world of manuscript fraktur art to the world of the broadside and the print. Beginning in the eighteenth century, some *taufschein* artists, such as Heinrich Otto of Lancaster County, went to country printers and ordered batches of blank birth and baptismal certificates. These they colored, filled in with the appropriate dates, and added freehand designs to as the spirit moved them. As the nineteenth century proceeded, these printed *taufscheins* became more and more numerous. They show a carry-over of folk motifs from the older European folk repertoire, but increasingly these are replaced or shoved aside by newer American motifs from the popular culture. These include the American eagle, the flag, the all-seeing eye, neoclassical urns and altars, and other aspects of national and stylish art. By the 1860s the printed *taufschein* forms had almost completely replaced the manuscript fraktur forms. The printed forms themselves had undergone an aesthetic transformation. They went Victorian, so to speak, with shaded romantic figures, wreaths, and floral arrangements. This was farewell to fraktur except for certain archaic pockets of fraktur production in Pennsylvania Dutch culture, the best example being the Old Order Amish and the Old Order Mennonites. Both of these ultra-conservative groups continued to decorate bookplates and inscribe fraktur family registers into their Bibles and other devotional books into the twentieth century.

The symbolic prints of the Pennsylvania Dutch are an important American example of the continuance on American soil of European folk and popular print motifs. Many of these prints that issued from the country presses and appeared on the walls of Pennsylvania farmhouses and taverns were based on European originals, making comparative studies of European prototypes a necessity. This is not to say that the American copies remained completely derivative. In the hands of clever engravers the European original took on definite American character.

One of the most talented publishers of broadsides and prints in all of America was the Harrisburg printer Gustavus Sigismund Peters (1793–1847). An emigrant from Saxony, Peters had in the 1820s set up a press in Carlisle, Pennsylvania, whence he removed to Harrisburg, the state capital.

verses that accompany the stages (and the entire format) appealed to the religious mind, hence such art as this could appropriately be framed for display upon the walls of the homes of religiously oriented farmers and craftsmen. The entire piece is a sophisticated "memento mori" such as was popular in many forms in the Victorian era.

Somewhat more weighted toward traditional theology with its rewards and punishments is the graphic "Two Ways" print by Peters. This shows the "broad way that leadeth to destruction" (Matthew 7)—and graphically depicts a gaping cavern of hell flaming with eternal fires of retribution. Rising above it is the "narrow way that leadeth unto life." Like many manuscript fraktur pieces, this print is oriented with an earth side and a heaven side, the heaven side in this case being the "New Jerusalem," the spiritual heaven from the book of Revelation. Traditional symbols—sun, moon, and stars—also adorn this piece. In a sense, the Two Ways is a drawing of the spiritual universe, portraying the ancient dualism between Satan and Christ, Heaven and Hell, with struggling man caught in the realm of choice between them. It was immensely popular and went through many editions, offered for sale by Peters as well as other early Pennsylvania Dutch printers.

Traue—Schaue—Wem? (Trust—Show—To Whom?). Woodcut with letterpress, on wove paper; 40.5 × 33 cm (sheet). Imprint: Gedruckt und zu haben bey G.S. Peters, [Gustave Sigismund Peters]—Harrisburg, Pa. (LC-USZ62-93925)

His production was bilingual, German and English, and catered to the religious, occult, and secular tastes of the Pennsylvania Dutch clientele. From 1825 until his death he issued thousands of German books, pamphlets, chapbooks, broadsides, printed fraktur pieces, children's toy books, and, especially, allegorical and religious prints. For these he did his own engraving and his woodcuts are superb.

Among his prints are two that deserve detailed mention. The first is "Das Leben und Alter der Menschen," which shows the progress of human life from birth to death, from the cradle to the grave. The aging process is seen in the progressively conservative dress and the giving up of luxuries. The symbolic animal figures that represent the different ages are significant. The religious

There is one final question that we wish to ask. Are there no parallels to fraktur art in other American cultures? If we use my term *manuscript art* rather than the uniquely Pennsylvania Dutch term *fraktur,* the answer is yes. Fraktur is uniquely Pennsylvania Dutch, but manuscript art did develop in certain other early American ethnic and sectarian groups. The New England Puritans and other Anglo-Americans, including the Quakers, indulged in manuscript art, particularly decorated family registers, a permitted form of art in those cultures. Shaker art is another example. In the great spiritual awakening that rocked the Shaker world in mid-nineteenth century, manuscript art was produced in abundance using Shaker symbolism in what have been called both "spirit drawings" and "gift drawings." A third and last example out of the many that could be cited is the art of the Russian-German Mennonites who brought their mostly Holland Dutch and Low German cultural traditions from the steppes to the Great Plains in the 1870s. Their art, which has recently been analyzed, is more closely related to fraktur and involves what the Russian-Germans called *Zierschriften* or "ornamental writings."

The fraktur art of the Pennsylvania Dutch, has, since its discovery by the outside world in the late nineteenth century, taken its place as a central genre of American folk art. In the process it has become the most sought after of all forms of Pennsylvania Dutch artistic production. Collections are housed in major libraries and museums across the nation, and private collectors have assembled equally significant holdings.

Das Leben und Alter der Menschen (The Life and Ages of Mankind). Woodcut and letterpress on wove paper; 33 × 39.5 cm (sheet). Imprint: Carlisle, Pa.—Gedruckt und zu haben bey Moser und Peters.—1826. (LC-USZ62-93913)

Glass Painting by Plain People

BY ERVIN BECK

PHOTOGRAPHS BY JEFF HOCHSTEDLER

The Old Order Amish are the most iconoclastic heirs of the Zwinglian Reformation. The Swiss Brethren (Mennonites), who separated from Ulrich Zwingli in 1525, continued his ban on images in religious worship. The Amish, who separated from the Mennonites in 1693–97, have gone even further in rejecting pictorial art. Their literal interpretation of the Second Commandment, "Thou shalt not make thee any graven image," has led them to forgo the use of photography and to refuse to have themselves—and sometimes also their possessions—photographed by others. Historically, in their folk arts they refrain from depicting the human form and represent objects from nature in a highly stylized, rather than realistic, manner. The best example, of course, are antique Amish quilts, which are primarily of geometrical design.

Given such an image-denying culture, it is somewhat surprising that many Amish communities today support a tradition of pictorial folk art painted on glass in the form of mottos and commemorative records. True, the pictorial elements are usually flowers, birds, and butterflies that decorate moral statements rather than full-

Inside the Town Line Fabric Store, located between Goshen and Emma, Indiana, Katie Miller's mottos hang above a display of notions.

blown landscapes or other pictures presented as art for art's sake. But in light of the scarcity of pictorial wall-art in folk cultures in general, and given the traditional Amish suspicion of images, the continuing interest in painted glass offers an opportunity to study the role of folk art and folk artists in a culture that is suspicious of art for moral and religious reasons.

The photographs accompanying this essay illustrate three different glass-painting techniques. Most paintings shown here are called "tinsel" paintings in America. As shown in *Figures 1, 2,* and others, they are reverse paintings on glass with a tinfoil backing. First the artist outlines the design with india ink or black oil paint on the back side of the glass, and paints the background area with opaque paint. Then she paints some areas with colored opaque paints, other areas with translucent colored paint, and leaves some areas unpainted. Prior to about 1945, most backgrounds were black *(Figure 10)*; today, almost all are white.

Before the painting is framed, a sheet of crinkled foil is inserted between the painting and the cardboard backing. In earlier years, the foil came from discarded cigarette and gum wrappers; now it comes from rolls of aluminum foil. The foil backing shines silver through the unpainted areas and shiny-colored through the areas painted with translucent paint.

Since all paint is applied to the back side of the glass, the basic technique is known as reverse glass painting in English, *Hinterglasmalerei* (behind-glass-writing) in standard German, and *hinrich schreiva* (backward writing) or *hinna seit schreiva* (back side writing) in the Pennsylvania German dialect spoken as a native language by Amish glass painters. However, the term most commonly used by Amish for these paintings is *mottos*.

A second, more currently popular technique is illustrated by *Figures 8 and 9.* In these, text and pictorial elements are applied to the top side of the glass with tubes of liquid embroidery paint. An opaque background—sometimes white, often pastel—is sprayed onto the back side of the glass, sometimes with marbleized or shaded effects. The painting is then "framed" with

"ladder" chain, whose squarish links firmly grip all four edges of the glass.

A third technique, used by only a few artists, incorporates elements from the other two in a kind of composite medium. As in *Figure 7,* text and decorations are applied to the back side of the glass. No translucent paints are used. And in place of a sheet of tinfoil, the silvery effect is achieved by gluing bits of silver glitter on to certain areas. This makes it possible for the painting to be framed with ladder chain rather than with a conventional frame.

All three techniques result in paintings with glossy, sparkling surfaces. Because it is difficult to attain depth of field in glass painting, painted areas appear "flat," although in tinsel painting the crinkled foil backing adds some feeling of depth to the design.

Glass painting is an ancient art that originated, apparently, with the invention of glass making in ancient Syria. Its religious use in the West began with Christian portrait medallions such as those found in the catacombs of Rome, continued with glass-painted icons in Byzantium, and flourished as a fine art in the European Renaissance and Reformation. By 1700 paintings on glass for devotional purposes had become a popular art produced in glass-making centers in Germany, Slovakia, Austria, and elsewhere.

Catholic and Protestant uses differed significantly, however. Catholic paintings on glass depicted the human form, whether in portraits of the saints or in scenes from the Bible. They were typically displayed in the *Herrgottswinkel* (God's corner) of the house, a devotional area decorated with holy pictures and ceramic plates.

Protestant glass paintings in Europe normally eschewed the human form and most pictorial representation, presenting instead scriptural, moral, or historical writings in fine calligraphy, with occasional linear flourishes or floral decorations. European Protestants, especially Lutherans, typically hung these paintings in the "Bible corner" of the house, along with a portrait of Luther and other inducements to devotion. The Amish and Mennonite glass paintings presented here clearly fit within this tradition of design and function.

However, they are apparently *not* part of an unbroken continuity with these European paintings. Although some of the earliest Anabaptists were professional painters on glass, and although both the Amish and Mennonites came from Switzerland and Alsace, where glass painting flourished, there is no evidence to suggest that they brought this folk art with them from Europe and continued its manufacture in the United States. Instead, glass painting apparently emerged among them in America only since about 1930 as the result of various influences from popular, folk, and fine art of the early twentieth century.

First, of course, were other glass painting traditions in American culture. Chief among them were the Catholic and Protestant glass paintings made and used by other religious groups, particularly in German-speaking cultures. Amish and Mennonites must have seen—and occasionally even used—these paintings in their homes. Various glass-painting traditions were also present in English-speaking American culture. They include scenes painted on the glass of clock cases, lithographs converted to glass paintings in the China trade, romantic European landscapes apparently imported from Europe, and floral still lifes probably made at home by women during the nineteenth century.

The most important influence may have been instruction in the craft given to Amish and Mennonite students in elementary schools. The December 1930 issue of *The School Arts Magazine,* for instance, describes "How to Make Pictures Of Glorified Glass." The instructions yield a black silhouette scene backed with tinfoil and cardboard and framed with bookbinding (passe-partout) tape. One Mennonite teacher recalls being taught how to do tinsel painting in an elementary education course at Western Oregon University about 1934. She found it an attractive kind of project because it used readily available, inexpensive materials and kept her students busy over several days' time while the various colors of paint dried. I know of Mennonite teachers who taught this craft to Mennonite and Amish students in the 1930s in places as far-flung as Oregon, Indiana, and Maryland.

The way school craft became home-grown folk art is suggested by one Mennonite informant from Iowa who learned glass painting in public elementary school, taught her mother at home, and then watched her mother and aunt develop glass-painted mottos in a kind of friendly rivalry. The main difference between school and home art is that the school tradition was apparently entirely pictorial, whereas the home tradition almost invariably featured a motto or scripture text, with pictorial elements for decoration. Here we see again how folk artists borrow a technique from one context and then deliberately adapt it according to the tastes, needs, and values of another.

As school and home art, the technique was also supported by manufacturers of tinsel paintings and by craft supply houses, both of which served a nationwide market. As late as 1958 the catalog for Thayer and Chandler of Chicago urged readers to "Paint Glorified Glass Pictures for Profit. Popular—Easy to Do—Astonishing Results." It offered patterns for silhouettes and regular scenes (but no mottos) as well as supplies such as pieces of glass, oriental lacquers, glass emulsion for outlining, passe-partout tape, and picture frames. Apparently Thayer and Chandler was the major source of supplies for Amish and Mennonite painters on glass. When it discontinued the sale of oriental lacquers about twenty years ago, many glass painters stopped working.

Finally, twentieth-century glass painting in both popular art and folk art may have been inspired by developments in western fine art at the same time and a bit earlier. In the early 1900s, for instance, Wassily Kandinsky and Paul Klee, among others, revived reverse glass painting after being attracted by the bright, flat colors of European folk paintings on glass. A more influential revival occurred in the 1920s in France, during the Art Deco movement, when painters such as Rene Buthaud and Jean Dupas revived interest in the technique. Dupas's history of navigation, painted on glass for the salon of the ocean liner *Normandie* and now partly preserved in the restaurant area of the Metropolitan Museum of Art, is one monument to the revival of reverse painting on glass. It helps us see that both popular and folk uses of the medium were part of a widespread appreciation during the Art Deco period of flat, hard, glossy, decorative surfaces.

That may not be what one would normally expect from people otherwise committed to a "plain" aesthetic, but the fact remains that the painting of mottos and commemorative records in this glittering, showy medium was very popular among Mennonites and Amish from about 1930 to 1950. It continues today as a living, although much reduced, tradition among Amish folk artists in Lancaster and Mifflin Counties in Pennsylvania, near Macon, Mississippi, and especially in Lagrange and Elkhart Counties in Indiana, from which come all of the illustrations shown here.

The designs of these paintings represent "copyist" art, since they are not drawn free-hand but derive from pre-existing patterns—as do many other folk arts, of course, including the fraktur tradition in Pennsylvania German culture. Sometimes the copying of a pattern is strict, as when glass painters simply trace the design off a lithographed moral wall decoration. Usually, however, the process is more creative. Sometimes glass artists take a large single design from Thayer and Chandler and add a suitable text. Most boxes of glass-painting patterns that I have seen contain separate decorative elements (flowers, birds, flourishes) that can be combined in creative ways with various texts to form new paintings. Often, then, the patterns for these paintings are transmitted whole from artist to artist, although each new rendering is made unique by alterations in coloring, adjustments in the design to fit the size of

the frame being used, and minor rearrangements of text or decoration.

Some overall tendencies emerge in the hundreds of glass paintings that I have seen. First, pictorial elements are as prominent as verbal ones in Amish work. This contrasts to the earlier word-dominated Protestant paintings and is striking when one considers the general Amish suspicion of imagery. Second, the pictorial elements are almost always images from nature, especially birds, flowers, plants, and butterflies—nature in its smiling aspect. Full landscapes are rare, especially in Amish work, but more common in Mennonite work. The human figure is almost universally absent in Amish painting but sometimes present in Mennonite painting. And overt symbolism is generally lacking in Amish designs, although often present in Mennonite designs.

Even though the pictorial elements are impressive, this is essentially an art form dedicated to transforming verbal truth into beauty. In fact, the verbal element is so powerful that even in those rare instances where glass paintings lack words *(Figure 1)*, Amish artists invariably call them "mottos." Fine—usually fancy—lettering, therefore, is a criterion of achievement in such work, whether it follows Gothic, Spencerian, Hallmark, or newspaper banner styles.

Most of the texts are scripture passages, with the Lord's Prayer probably the most common. Following in popularity are moral and religious sayings, such as "Jesus Saves" or "Trust and Obey." In addition, glass paintings often display house blessings, praise of motherhood, statements of friendship, and, occasionally, popular secular verse.

A different category of glass paintings records family history. Marriage records, birth records, family genealogies, death memorials, and wedding anniversary records are common, as are birthday and Father's-and Mother's-Day greetings. Such records are made only by Amish, not by Mennonite, glass artists, probably because they take

Mary Miller's dining area contains six glass-door cupboards full of colorful plates and glassware, mostly antique. Six of Mary's glittering tinsel paintings fit in harmoniously with this glass-dominated decor. Here "The Lord's Prayer" dominates the sideboard and dining area of the room, offering a fitting devotional focus for mealtime. The kind and number of items permitted on the walls of houses depends upon the rules of each Amish district. Mary's district allows some mottos on the walls but not "great big paintings" or "scenery bought in the store."

the place of photographs in creating a permanent record of transitional rites for these picture-renouncing people.

In a fully documented article in *The Mennonite Quarterly Review* (April 1989) I discuss in greater detail much of the above and also speculate on what glass painting communicates about the changing aesthetics, culture, sociology, and theology of the Amish. In the remainder of this essay and in

the captions for the illustrations included here, I focus on the lives and work of five living glass artists in order to show how, by whom, and to what effect such folk art is produced in these "plain" communities. Although this survey of artists focuses on the dynamic, contemporary human element of the tradition, it also implies a great deal in regard to the topics mentioned above but not dealt with directly in this article.

The tinsel paintings of Mary Miller (b. 1931) are among the most interesting from the Amish community because of their careful execution, creative design, and large size (her peacock, *Figure 1,* is 20 in. × 23 in.). Mary learned tinsel painting when she was seventeen years old from Mary Christner (1897–1979), a Mennonite who managed the Honeyville general store. Following her marriage, she also began making commemorative family records in the medium. Between 1948 and 1975, when she quit because of weakened eyesight, she made 219 paintings for Amish throughout the Midwest at prices ranging from one to fifteen dollars.

Mary's work was highly collaborative. At first, she worked with her sister-in-law Katie Miller Schlabach (b. 1932), with whom she developed and traded patterns. Both Mary and Katie used the help of Katie's mother Anna J., who was known for her fine handwriting. In making family records, they usually asked Anna to do the handwriting patterns for them. In exchange, they did baking for her or helped with housecleaning. Later, Mary enlisted the help of her husband and children in designing patterns, doing careful handwriting, and helping with repetitious painting.

In addition to teaching others the craft, Mary has been a conservator of the art in other ways. For instance, she chose to continue to do tinsel painting when painting on top of glass became more popular in her community. Also, she remains actively interested in her daughter's tinsel painting and exerts a conservative influence over her. When her daughter was thinking of using a new design for a birth announcement, Mary said something like, "Oh, I'd use this one instead," and her daughter has been using the old design ever since.

Figure 1. PEACOCK: This striking painting of a peacock is unusual in many ways. Mary Miller got the pattern for it from her teacher, Mary Christner, who kept peacocks in the yard of the Honeyville store. Although the pattern may originally have come from an embroidered dresser scarf, it is related to images from much earlier Pennsylvania German folk art, in which the peacock was a traditional image in fraktur work and the design of classical columns supporting an arch was found on many decorated blanket chests. It is also one of the few Amish tinsel paintings without a motto. Why? "You know, I've always wondered myself," Mary says. Despite the painting's lack of words, Mary still calls it a "motto."

Mary is unaware of the ancient association of the peacock with the phoenix and, in turn, of the phoenix with the resurrected Christ. The peacock apparently has a less noble meaning in Amish culture. As Mary's husband recalls, "We had a preacher when I was a kid. He was from Kansas and he said, 'Now, just like a peacock. He goes and struts, you know. And you'd tell him he isn't as pretty as he thinks he is. Just look at your dirty feet!'" Amish preachers sometimes refer in their sermons to mottos hanging on the walls of the house in which a Sunday worship service is being held. Since Mary's peacock hung in a bedroom rather than the living room, it may have escaped being used as an object lesson in humility.

Figure 2. MARRIAGE RECORD: Mary Miller's marriage record design came from her sister-in-law, who adapted it from a late-nineteenth-century printed wedding record. Mary's son created the open book shapes to replace the ovals from the lithograph. Mary added the bow to the design. Mary's mother-in-law added "Peace be unto you," borne by the bird, and also created the lettering with the squiggles below and above the text "to make it look a little fancier."

The Amish marriage record retains all the text of the original but adds a section for "table-waiters" at the bottom. In Amish weddings, friends of the bride and groom are asked to wait on tables during the wedding reception and are regarded as official members of the wedding party. Such wedding records are often gifts from parents to the newlyweds and are first publicly displayed behind the *Eck,* or corner table, where the wedding party sits during the wedding reception.

Figure 2

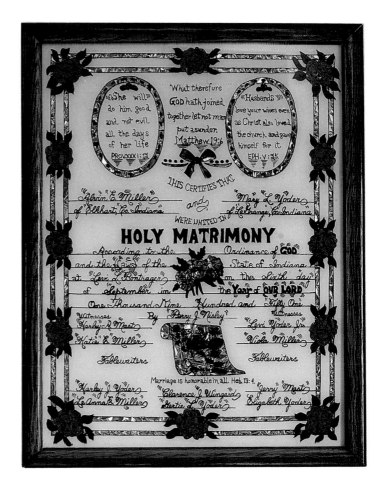

Figure 1

Figure 3

Figure 4

Figures 3 and 4. THE LORD'S PRAYER AND PRINTED ORIGINAL: This is the favorite motto of Mary's family. "I doubt it if money can buy that," says her husband. It was a wedding gift to them from his sister Katie, who adapted the design from a nineteenth-century lithograph of the Lord's Prayer, shown here beside her painting. Katie's pattern preserves the print's layout of the text but adds entirely different decorations. In place of the Ten Commandments (with human subjects) that surround the lithographed text, the Amish artists have added a bow and images from nature—birds, flowers, foliage, and butterflies. This is the most ubiquitous tinsel-painting design in Northern Indiana.

Katie Schmucker Miller (b. 1956) began tinsel painting in April 1986 because she wanted to earn some extra money. The mother of five children fourteen years old and younger, Katie lives in the small village of Emma in Lagrange County. She learned the rudiments of tinsel painting by spending a day with her teacher at her aunt's house, then having the teacher come to her own house for a day.

Although her teacher had inherited all of Mary Miller's patterns, Katie borrowed only a few from her. She has made most of her own patterns. She gets most of the design elements from her mother's collection of quilt block and embroidery patterns. She also uses pictures from coloring books published for Amish children. Yet despite the innovative nature of her work, it remains very traditional in its use of texts and designs.

Like Mary Miller, Katie also relies heavily on collaboration with family and friends. Friends help her by finding inexpensive frames for her at garage sales. Her brother sometimes makes frames, and her sister does all of the lettering. In fact, once a week Katie meets with her sister at her mother's house in order to give her sister the orders for the next week and collect the letter designs that she requested of her previous week.

Figure 5

Katie markets her work in many ways. She uses some paintings as birthday and friendship gifts. Family and friends order mottos directly from her. She sells some at other people's garage sales. She places others at Amish country stores operated by her friends or relatives. The farthest she has gone in marketing her paintings beyond the Amish community is the Galarina Arts store in Shipshewana, which caters to tourists. But even there they were sold mainly to Amish customers, which indicates that, despite the current American craze for "folk art," the taste for tinsel mottos has not moved beyond the Amish community.

In her first four months of glass painting, Katie sold fifty mottos. Her work represents the most vigorous continuation of tinsel painting, and it will be interesting to see if her efforts will reinstate it in her community as the widely patronized folk art that it once was.

Figure 5. TEN COMMANDMENTS: "The Ten Commandments" is one of the most popular and elaborate of Katie Miller's mottos. She copied the script from a print version but added flowers of her own choosing, apparently from an embroidery design. Katie uses deeply crinkled foil behind her paintings, which gives them a more three-dimensional effect than is found in the work of other artists.

The Town Line Fabric Store, located between Goshen and Emma, sells Katie Miller's glass mottos on consignment. The owner of the store, which has a largely Amish clientele, is Katie's cousin.

Figure 7

IN LOVING REMEMBRANCE OF
SISTER
SUSIE BONTRAGER
BORN.....OCTOBER 4, 1948
DIED.....JULY 16, 1975
AGE...26 YRS. 9 MOS. 12 DAYS

Gone but not forgotten

MEMORIES ARE TREASURES
NO ONE CAN STEAL
DEATH IS A HEARTACHE
ONLY GOD CAN HEAL.

Dearest Sister she has left us
Left us, yes, for evermore
But we hope to meet our loved one
On that bright and happy shore.

Lonely the house and sad the hours
Since our dear one has gone
But, oh a brighter home than ours
In Heaven, is now her own.

O how we miss you "Sister" dear
As you quietly sleep and rest
But we think of your home in Heaven
And we know that God knows best.

As we loved you, so we miss you
In our memory you are dear
Loved, remembered, thought of always
Brings many a silent tear.

Figure 6

THIS IS
THE DAY
THE LORD
HATH
MADE,
Ps. 118:24

Sarah Ellen Troyer (b. 1940) is an unmarried Amish woman who supports herself by making patterns for new cloth products in the mobile home industry. From 1962 until 1983 Sarah Ellen made glass mottos for her Amish community. She apparently originated the composite glass-painting technique described above.

Sarah Ellen learned painting on top of glass from her Conservative Mennonite neighbor, Mary Bontrager, who once gave her a small motto, "What a Friend We Have in Jesus," for helping her with spring housecleaning. Sarah Ellen soon became a major supplier of mottos for her community. She made over five hundred such mottos, sometimes as many as one hundred per year. At the peak of her production, she was ordering one hundred dollars worth of ladder chain at a time. In fact, orders were so heavy that what started out to be a hobby for her eventually became a chore. "I always felt obligated to do it," Sarah Ellen

says. When she felt that she absolutely must quit painting on glass, she found that she could not merely say no and stop. Instead, she says, "I made sure I was out of chain and I started saying no."

Figure 7. DEATH RECORD: This death record blends the techniques of tinsel painting and painting on top of glass. The verses come from the obituary section of *The Budget,* the weekly newspaper published in Sugarcreek, Ohio, that serves the international Amish community. Although the design comes from Mary Miller's pattern box, it ultimately derives from memorial cards prepared by an Amish printer in Pennsylvania for Amish customers throughout the United States.

Figure 6. NEW STYLE MOTTO: No regulations forbid Amish use of new household crafts as they become popular in mainstream American culture. They now make mottos and family records in woodburning, velvet painting, shadow box, and other faddish media. Here Sarah Ellen Troyer adapts the motto tradition to painting on wood decorated with a dried bouquet.

Waneta Miller (b. 1968) has had a typical glass-painting career for an Amish woman. In 1982 she completed eight grades of education, four in public school and four in her district's Amish school. When she stopped going to school, she took up glass painting, both as a diversion and as a means of earning money. Actually, she was asked to learn the craft by Sarah Ellen Troyer, and Waneta eagerly accepted the offer. Sarah Ellen and Waneta are neighbors and Waneta's parents used to sell Sarah Ellen's mottos in Miller's Country Store, which they operate in a separate, garage-like building behind their house.

The demand for Waneta's mottos is greater than she can supply. She gives away many for Christmas, birthday, and wedding gifts. She frequently receives orders for

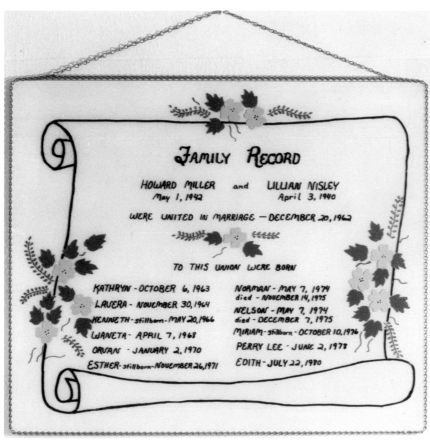

Figure 8

Figure 9

multiple copies of the same item—as from a Conservative Mennonite Bible School teacher for all of her students and from parents who order the same motto as a gift for all of their children. At Christmas time she is unable to fill all the orders she receives. Waneta also supplies mottos for sale in her parents' store, but they have been forced by demand to augment their stock by purchasing glass mottos by mail from a woman in Pennsylvania.

After making about three hundred mottos in three years, in 1986 Waneta stopped making them in large quantities and now makes them only for special occasions. She quit because the demand was so high and because she made too little profit to justify continuing the work as a leisure-time activity. She was relieved when her cousins became interested in learning the art and taking over her business.

When I asked Waneta if she ever signed her name on a motto, she replied, "People don't have to know who made it." To which her mother added, "Artists do. But actually this is just copying a pattern." They could think of no word in their Pennsylvania German dialect for art, and had to resort to a dictionary to find the standard German equivalent, *Kunst*. To them, art means freehand drawing—"the kind found in museums."

Figure 8. DANKET DEM HERRN: The translation of this motto painted on top of glass is, "O thank the Lord, for he is good, and his mercy endures." It is the favorite motto of Waneta's customers. The verse is used in almost every worship service in her Amish district. Glass mottos written in German are unusual, since the Amish speak a German dialect that has no conventional written form and are often unable to read much standard German.

Figure 9. FAMILY RECORD: The scroll design is a typical one for Amish genealogies painted on top of glass. It takes Waneta Miller a full day to make a family record like this. Although it looks like the technique of painting on top of glass, on this record all of the design is painted on the back side instead.

Loyal Ressler (b. 1929) of rural Nappanee, Indiana, is a Conservative Mennonite farmer and tinsel painter. He did most of his painting on glass between 1953 and 1956, when he was working in the kitchen of the Irene Byron Hospital in Fort Wayne. As a conscientious objector to military service, he had gone there to fulfill his government requirement of alternative civilian service—called "1-W work," after the Selective Service category assigned to men granted C.O. status by their draft boards. While living in close fellowship with the many kinds of Mennonites and Amish who were there doing the same kind of work, Loyal learned glass painting and produced hundreds of mottos for the 1-W men and their families who came to visit them.

"I sold and sold and sold to 1-W's and Mennonite people," he says. "People would think it foolish to have pictures on the wall. Pictures wouldn't have gone over at all. That's why these mottos took very well." Loyal's mottos are a logical extension of his commitment to evangelical Christianity: "When I became a Christian, I went into spiritual things—that would have a meaning for people."

Loyal even made some mottos for Mennonite meetinghouses in the Fort Wayne area. Bearing verses such as "Let the Lord Be Magnified" and "This is the House of the Lord," these mottos were hung on the front wall of the sanctuaries of these churches—near the attendance board that used to dominate every Mennonite pulpit area—as inducements to worship.

Following the interest I have shown in his work, Loyal has once again brought out his homemade light box and patterns and has

Loyal and Norma Jean Ressler stand in front of a Conservative Mennonite Church building near their home. The "plain" suit that Loyal wears here is customary dress for Sundays and other formal occasions, by lay as well as ordained members in his congregation.

Figure 10

found craft paints to substitute for the oriental lacquers that he once used. But he still has a large box full of unused, unsold mottos that he made long ago. And it is unlikely that his paintings will find ready acceptance today among his fellow Conservative Mennonites, who are now more interested in paintings on velvet and, indeed, in the "foolish pictures" that they earlier condemned.

Figure 10. LOVE ONE ANOTHER: This is a very typical design for a tinsel painting motto. The black background is typical of Protestant mottos made by reverse glass painting since the early Reformation. It was also typical for Indiana and Amish glass paintings until about 1945. Since then, white backgrounds have become the norm.

Figure 11. LET THE LORD BE MAGNIFIED: Loyal Ressler made this motto for the Anderson Mennonite Church near Fort Wayne, which he attended and where it hung for many years. The meetinghouse drawn in the insert is based on a picture of the First Mennonite Church of Fort Wayne printed on its Sunday bulletin.

Figure 11

"New" Pots for Old

Burlon Craig's Strategy for Success

BY CHARLES G. ZUG III

I well remember the first time I met Burlon Craig. It was late January of 1977, a clear, cold winter evening, when I drove into his yard and saw the weathered frame shop, the huge groundhog kiln, and the shed full of alkaline-glazed stoneware. For several years, I had been doing research on the traditional potters of North Carolina and had heard occasional reports of an "old-time" potter who was still at work somewhere in rural Lincoln County in the western piedmont. And so, with the help of Tom and Asa Blackburn, whose father and grandfather had also worked in the craft, I finally tracked Burl down. And what a find he was. As he took me on a quick tour of his pottery that evening, it seemed as though I had leapt back at least half a century, to another era when there were a dozen similar shops here, all producing sturdy vessels for use in local homes and farms. At the same time, there was a note of sadness. Burl had not burned his kiln for several months, yet there were numerous unsold churn-jars, milk crocks, and flowerpots in his storage shed. And the prices were so modest—even the five-gallon churn-jars, which were a full eighteen inches high and probably held closer to six gallons, cost only seven dollars. Surely, I thought, this was the end of a great tradition, the waning years of a fine craftsman's life. I was wrong.

It is now ten years later, June 30, 1987, to be exact, a hot, humid Carolina summer morning. At eight o'clock there are approximately 130 people in the Craigs' front yard, all of them straining at the rope that holds them back from the five hundred pieces of glimmering stoneware spread out on the grass at the end of the kiln. Burl's wife Irene, who handles most of the sales, finally gives the signal, and the impatient crowd surges forward. What follows is ten minutes of frenzy, as the buyers elbow, argue, and assemble their collections of pots. There are no seven dollar five-gallon churn-jars in this lot; the price is now one hundred dollars for the same piece, and no one complains. Then Irene and Burl move in to settle accounts and help pack the wares. Perhaps two hours later, the yard is clear once again, of both people and pots. Only a few culls remain—a face jug with a nose missing, a pitcher with a cracked rim, a vase with an underfired glaze. These are placed in the now largely empty storage shed, where, within the next few weeks, some late-comer will be happy to purchase them.

Perhaps no one is more surprised at this newfound prosperity than Burl Craig himself. As he often observes, he may now receive more money for a single pot than he once did for an entire kilnful. And the last decade has brought much more than just a sizeable income. His wares have been featured in numerous exhibitions, both within the state and without. He has performed at the Smithsonian's Festival of American Folklife on the National Mall in Washington and the World's Fair in Knoxville. Scarcely a month passes in which Burl's life and work are not celebrated in some newspaper, magazine, or book. Finally, in 1984 he and Irene journeyed again to Washington to receive a National Heritage Fellowship from the National Endowment for the Arts. One of seventeen traditional artists so honored, Burl received a five thousand dollar award, a silver medal, and a citation

signed by the president of the United States. No longer a virtual unknown in his own state, Burl now possesses a national reputation. In part, his success has stemmed from trends beyond his control: the celebration of the Bicentennial; the popular obsession with "country" objects; and the academic interest in material culture and folklife studies. But Burl himself has played the major role in the renewal of his craft, by recognizing the interests of his new customers and altering his repertory to suit them. His rise to fame and fortune is due as much to his own efforts as to external forces of change.

Burlon Craig and a harvest of wares fresh from the kiln, Catawba County, North Carolina. Photograph by Charles Zug, 1978

Burlon B. Craig was born on April 21, 1914, and lived with his family on a small farm in Catawba County, a mile or so north of his present location. His father was a farmer, carpenter, and preacher, and so, like most young children, Burl spent much of his youth working in the fields or doing the daily chores essential to farm life. Burl attended the local schools but readily admits he didn't like to go; furthermore, his family frequently took him out, particularly in the spring to help with the plowing. By the first grade, however, he had discovered another interest—the pottery shop of Lawrence Leonard, which was all too conveniently close to the school. As Burl recalls, "We'd run off from school and go down and watch Will Bass turn—from the old Ridge Academy schoolhouse down there. . . . We got an hour then at noon, let out an hour at school, you know, why I'd go down there. And sometimes I'd run off and go down there, watching them turn. That fascinated me."[1] Lawrence Leonard and Will Bass were not the only potters that young Burl Craig could "study." There were numerous other shops in the immediate vicinity, producing utilitarian alkaline-glazed stoneware and carrying on a craft that began in the late eighteenth or early nineteenth century. Altogether, at least 150 potters are known to have worked in this Catawba Valley tradition, which extends

along the western end of the common border between Lincoln and Catawba Counties.[2]

Although early absorbed in the potter's art, Burl did not get his hands into the clay until he was about fourteen. He had been cutting cordwood on his father's land, and his labors attracted the eye of veteran potter Jim Lynn. "One day I was down in the woods there cutting wood, and he wanted to know if I wouldn't go in with him now, as partners, in the pottery business. I said, 'How do you want to work that, Jim?' He said, 'Well,' said, 'I'll give you half the profit. . . . I'll do the turning till you learn.' And says, 'We'll use this wood!'" Jim was in his late fifties by this time and had no one to help him. Moreover, as Burl adds with a sly grin, he "didn't have no money to buy no wood with!" (Interview, Aug. 21, 1981). Even though he knew Jim coveted his woodpile, Burl recognized the value of the proposal. "I said, 'Now I'll do this, Jim, I'll try it. And if I'm not able to turn something or make a little money out of it by next spring, cotton planting time, I'll have to stop and help my daddy farm.' And by the next spring I was turning out some saleable stuff. I wasn't the best turner in the world,

but, you know, I was setting my stuff out with him, with Jim, and selling it—two gallon jars, three gallon churns, stuff like that" (Interview, Dec. 16, 1978). Clearly the theme of economic necessity runs through Burl's account. He *had* to make money at the craft; otherwise it was back to cotton farming with his father. But at the same time, this was more than just another job. "I never will forget the first two-gallon churn I turned and set it out with Jim's. I never will forget that as long as I live. I was really proud of that" (Interview, Aug. 21, 1981). The same pride and personal satisfaction remain in Burl's work some sixty years later.

After his apprenticeship with Jim Lynn, Burl worked throughout the thirties as a journeyman at potteries all across the region. Business was still quite strong during this period, and it was not unusual to turn out a kiln a week, particularly during the spring and fall, when wares were most in demand. Sometimes Burl turned for another potter, such as Harvey and Enoch Reinhardt or Uncle Seth Ritchie, and received the going rate of two cents per gallon. At other times he formed a partnership with another man and rented an unused shop. The forms he made were overtly utilitarian—mostly churns, jars, milk crocks, pitchers—and were sold according to their size, the normal rate being ten cents per gallon. This was a pragmatic, no-frills world, and Burl has never forgotten the advice he received while working with Floyd Hilton. "'Don't make any difference,' [he] said, 'Just so they hold what they're supposed to and got a good glaze on it.' Said, 'People's gonna set 'em in the smokehouse or cellar, and nobody'll ever see 'em anyway'" (Interview, July 10, 1981). Money was scarce, and so people wanted cheap, sturdy containers to process and store their foods. The aesthetics of the pot—its formal beauty or decoration—had little meaning in this eminently practical world. If twenty-five one-gallon jugs came out of the same kiln, they all sold for a dime—provided of course, that each had a smooth glaze and held a full gallon of vinegar or molasses or whiskey.

Still, there were changes occurring during Burl's journeyman years. The demand for the old forms was gradually declining. Prohibition had already drastically eroded the call for whisky jugs (except in Wilkes County). Commercial dairies and refrigerators were rendering the churn and milk crock obsolete. And factory-produced containers such as the fruit jar or tin can were slowly replacing the traditional storage vessels. At the same time, tourists, particularly from the mountain resorts, had gradually begun to discover the craftsmen in the Catawba Valley. Some of the more farsighted potters had begun to produce decorative

Burl Craig trimming the walls of a five-gallon churn-jar. Photograph by Charles Zug

forms with colored glazes, miniatures, and what was locally referred to as "swirl ware," a striped body made by mixing light and dark clays. But for every face jug or swirl vase, the potters still made twenty jars or milk crocks.

World War II largely ended the Catawba Valley tradition. Potters like Harvey Reinhardt went to work in the shipyard in Wilmington; others like Burl Craig joined the Navy. In 1945 he returned and purchased Harvey's shop, kiln, and home for $3,500. He found that most of the other potters were now gone or retired. Enoch Reinhardt, Harvey's brother, burned his last kiln in 1946 and turned his attention to his farm and barbershop. Poley Hartsoe closed his shop in 1957, leaving Burl to carry on alone. And carry on he has—except for a job in a furniture factory in Long Beach, California, 1959–60, Burl has made pottery continuously since 1945. "I made some all along. . . . Some years there I didn't make an awful lot, but I still made it. I'd say I was going to quit, and I'd work at something else a while, and then my old hands would get itching, and I'd be back in the clay yet" (Interview, Jan. 2, 1980).

For a time Burl just farmed and made pottery, as he had done during the thirties, but the boll weevil and capricious weather took their toll on his cotton and corn and wiped out his money crops. All that was left, Burl explains, was the "pottery to get the money out of, and I wasn't getting enough out of it to make a living out of it, so I got a job and worked at that too" (Interview, Dec. 28, 1984). In the mid-fifties he began working in area furniture factories to supplement his income. His longest stint was nineteen years at the North Hickory Furniture Company (1960–79). Still, he used his spare time to make three, four, sometimes six kilnfuls a year. The children were there to help—the Craigs have three sons and two daughters—and Irene could light off the kiln and tend it by herself until Burl got home in the evening. Then, together, they would "blast off" the kiln, jamming the fireboxes with wood to drive the temperature up to the full twenty-four hundred degrees Fahrenheit needed to mature the alkaline glaze. Since his prices were low

and he was the only remaining potter, Burl found he "could sell everything I made, mostly here. Even back when I was making just jars and milk crocks. The stores would come and pick them up" (Interview, Jan. 2, 1980). And, of course, the local people would use his wares for "home brew, wine, and pickles, and sauerkraut, stuff like that" (Interview, Dec. 28, 1984). But, by the mid-1970s, his traditional markets were drying up, and the future looked bleak. Fortunately, this was the period when Burl was gradually "discovered"—by academics like myself, by a growing horde of pottery collectors, and then by the dealers, some of whom successfully recycled his wares as old. Burl's response to his new clientele has been very perceptive. He has revived numerous old forms and created some new ones; he has increasingly emphasized deco-

ration; and he has been willing to sculpt faces on just about anything.

Throughout his journeyman years in the 1930s, Burl's repertory of forms was very limited. Most of the customers needed food storage vessels, and so Burl turned large numbers of churns, jars, and milk crocks. During the same period, potters also began making the churn-jar, a versatile hybrid that incorporated the characteristics of the old jar (wide shoulder) as well as the churn (relatively vertical form and flaring rim with an internal flange for the lid). Less commonly requested were pitchers, jugs, and flowerpots. Finally, for special orders he might produce rabbit feeders, chamber-

clientele of the 1970s was to revive old forms that were part of his inactive repertory, as well as others he had seen but never made himself. Two curious versions of the familiar jug form that have had great appeal are the ring jug and the monkey jug. The former is an old European type, and was made in small quantities by the early North Carolina potters, probably as a novelty or to display their virtuosity on the wheel. The monkey jug, on the other hand, may have Afro-American roots and usually appears as a single container with two canted spouts and a transverse strap handle. In the Catawba Valley, potters made their own version by piggybacking two separate containers, each with its own spout. This local form probably developed in the 1920s or the 1930s.[3] Burl asserts that "they were tourist things—they didn't have no practical use. Just a novelty. They always said, one was to put your whiskey in, one to keep your chaser in. . . . Fact is, I've never seen one with liquor and chaser in it"(Interview, Jan. 6, 1982). Other wares that Burl has revived are the barrel, the multi-spouted "quintal" or flower jug, the spittoon, the chicken waterer, even a grave marker. On occasion he will imitate a specific form or glaze by one of the early masters in the Catawba Valley. Specifically, he has made copies of jars and jugs by Daniel Seagle, who was the finest turner the region ever produced. In all such work, Burl has been able to produce a "history" of the Catawba Valley pottery, one that is tangible and obviously appeals to collectors (and people writing books on folk pottery) who are otherwise unable to find—or pay for—these archaic forms.

Burl has also introduced a number of new forms, but hardly as many as one might expect. For example, he now makes graduated sets of cannisters, which are handy in modern kitchens. These, however, are really just little churn-jars, with pottery lids like those once made for the preserve jars in the region. He also makes a variety of sinuous vases or lamp bases, but again these are simply variations on the ovoid jugs and jars he has always made. Then, there are the miniature versions of the traditional wares, little jars, jugs, pitchers, and

pots, or stove thimbles, the latter serving to insulate a metal stovepipe where it ran through the wall of the house. After the war, Burl specialized in churn-jars and milk crocks, adding some unglazed flowerpots, strawberry planters, and birdhouses to fill the cooler areas of the kiln, along the sides and in the chimney, where his alkaline glaze would not mature.

One of his first innovations for the new

them because they want a work of sculpture, a piece of "fine art" for their mantels, not a plain, old, useful jug. And for Burl, the face vessels are more efficient—like the swirl ware, they take up no more room in the kiln but command a higher price. As Burl sees it, making face vessels "is getting old, but what I like is the money I get out of it" (Interview, Aug. 19, 1983).

Clearly there is good money in the pottery business today, but that is probably the least important reason for Burl's continued adherence to the craft. For nearly half a century he "gave his pottery away" as he likes to put it, but he kept at it, even when forced to work in a factory. "I didn't want to quit—no, I like to make pottery, I like it. But . . . after World War II things had changed so it took more money to live, and I did have to get a job and work. But I still stayed with the pottery" (Interview, Dec. 28, 1984). Burl's father was a skilled carpenter, so it is not surprising that he chose a furniture factory. Most of the time Burl operated a cut-off saw to cut the lumber into appropriate lengths for the chairs, tables, beds, whatever was in production. Burl is a friendly, open sort of person, and he enjoyed the people he worked with but not the work itself. "You didn't get the same satisfaction like if you made a nice piece of pottery and stand back: 'Well, I done that myself.' When you made a chair, they was hundreds of people work on it. . . . You couldn't say, 'Oh, I made that chair,' like you could with a piece of pottery. When you turned that [pot] out, why that's something that you made individually. You made that yourself—you can take a little pride in that. But I never thought [that] of, like, making a chair, that I had very little to do with actually. It was just more or less a job, something to make a little money" (Interview, Dec. 28, 1984). What was lacking was the pride in individual creativity, in controlling the total process, he first felt as a boy when he set out his churns and jars with his mentor Jim Lynn.

In nurturing his craft through difficult

much more for a face vessel. In the old days, however, few people were willing to pay more than the standard rate of ten cents per gallon just to have ears, eyes, and teeth on their water jugs. Burl often affirms that he has no love for this lengthy decorating process—he much prefers turning the jug itself—but he knows he must respond to modern tastes. Burl has also produced a fair number of snake jugs, again at the request of collectors. These are much easier to make—he rolls out one or two clay snakes and then wraps them around the body of the pot. A few such vessels were made in the North in the nineteenth century as part of the temperance movement, but there has never been any such tradition in North Carolina. Making snake or face vessels does make good sense today. Collectors desire times, Burl has demonstrated a remarkable versatility and understanding. He adapted to changing economic conditions by moving from farm to factory work. And although raised in a world that demanded inexpensive, undecorated, utilitarian objects, he has perceptively recognized changing tastes and thus renewed the market for his pottery, which is now made to be seen, not just used. This does not mean gaudy colors or elaborate decoration. On the contrary, his efforts to heighten the visual appeal of his work are restrained and largely within traditional boundaries. For example, Burl explains, "On my five-gallon stuff I put four handles, most of it, instead of two anymore." There is no practical need for the extra handles (though the old potters like Daniel Seagle routinely put four handles on their massive ten- to twenty-gallon storage jars). Burl adds them "just for looks—lots of people want them. Sell better. Then I can put the glass on the

handle, each handle, and that gives me more streaks down [the sides]" (Interview, Dec. 28, 1984). In like manner, Burl not only makes many graceful vases and grinning face jugs, he makes them out of swirl, thereby multiplying their visual appeal for the buyer. Ultimately, it is a matter of degree or intensity—Burl remains within the Catawba Valley tradition but uses a greater number of decorative techniques on each pot than he would have earlier.

Occasionally, a writer will refer to Burl as an "artist" or a "master potter," or call his old shop his "studio." Such references amuse him. Despite his fame and popularity, Burl remains a profoundly modest man who enjoys the humorous incongruities between such easy journalistic labels and the realities of his work. In fact, another key to his success is his continued reliance on the technology of his predecessors. He still digs his clay by hand from bottomland on the South Fork of the Catawba River and

Burl and Irene Craig surrounded by some of their wares. Photograph by Charles Zug

trucks it back to his shop to weather. Next, he grinds it to the proper consistency in his clay mill, though he does now power it with his tractor instead of the once ubiquitous mule. From there the clay moves directly into the shop, where he turns the pots on his homemade treadle wheel, pumping the flywheel peddle with his left foot as he pulls up the clay walls with his hands. His glazes, as already noted, are concocted from local materials and then ground in a hand-powered stone glaze mill, a miniature of the old grist mills that once dotted the landscape. Finally, he burns his wares in his big groundhog kiln, a task that requires nearly three cords of pine slabs and ten hours of hard, hot work. In making few concessions to modernity, Burl firmly maintains his place in the long line of Catawba Valley potters.

Perhaps it is this adherence to traditional methods that is most important to his new-found prosperity. Buyers today are out to purchase a piece of history as well as a work of art. For this reason, they insist that he stamp all his pots with his name, as if to validate their character. When I first met Burl he had no stamp and rarely ever signed his pottery—now he even marks the miniatures with B. B. CRAIG / VALE, N.C. The importance of the man is manifested in the many anecdotes that circulate about his advanced age, or even his demise. One of Burl's favorites concerns the couple who appeared in his front yard one day. "I was mowing the yard, and they kept looking at me, kept looking. And directly he said to Irene, 'He don't *look* like he's eighty years old!' And Irene said, 'He's *not!*' [He] had been told by someone, 'If you want a piece of his, you better get it.' Says, 'He's eighty years old.' Says, 'He won't make much longer!'" (Interview, Dec. 28, 1984).

After a mild heart attack several years ago, Burl wisely halved his output to three kilns per year, one each in the spring, summer, and fall. Still in excellent health, he probably *will* go on making ware until he is eighty. If there is a single term for his strategy for survival and enormous success—over the last decade, it is probably conservatism. In effect, Burl's "innovation" has been to rely all the more on tradition, whether in forms, glazes, decoration, or technology. Granted, he has a much larger repertory today than ever before, and his wares are, on average, smaller and more colorful, but virtually everything he does is grounded in some way in the two-hundred-year-old Catawba Valley tradition. Thus, it is not surprising that he frequently thinks back to the old men who preceded him. "I tell you them Seagles was about the best potters that's ever been in this country in my book. I don't know of anybody yet that's got 'em beat. I know I've not." Burl's appraisal is typically modest and full of respect for the old masters. And it is with typical generosity that he regrets they are not here to share his achievement. "You know, sometimes I just get to studying. I sort of hate that some of them old people wasn't still a-living to see what it amounted to. They worked at it all their lives and didn't have anything, didn't make anything out of it. I just wished they could have lived to see it like it is today" (Interview, Dec. 28, 1984).

NOTES

1. Tape-recorded interview, Henry, North Carolina, December 16, 1978. All subsequent interview dates will be placed in the text in parentheses. *Turn* and *burn* are the Southern terms for throwing and firing pottery, and will be used throughout the essay.

2. For a full consideration of the Catawba Valley tradition, *see* Charles G. Zug III, *Turners and Burners: The Folk Potters of North Caro-* lina (Chapel Hill: University of North Carolina Press, 1986), chapter 3.

3. *See* Zug, 378–81.

4. On the "conspicuous consumption" (Thorstein Veblen's term) of modern crafts, *see* Susan L. F. Isaacs, "Retrospective Tradition: Potters and Buyers in the Contemporary Redware Marketplace," *New Jersey Folklife* 11 (1986): 29.

Plastic Strap Baskets

Containers for a Changing Context

BY SALLY PETERSON

"Sometimes, you know, my father, I think he's crazy," Mai Chue Lor said to me. "He keeps me awake with the light on, you know? Till two or three o'clock in the morning. Making those baskets."[1]

The baskets that so madden fifteen-year-old Mai Chue are made from discarded strips of plastic coil strapping. Her father, Chia Ker Lor, is a respected elder in Philadelphia's Laotian Hmong community. Several years ago, I became one of Chia Ker Lor's English tutors under the auspices of a local English as a Second Language program. I arrived one day to find him cutting lengths of garden hose, which he used to fashion handles on a basket woven from plastic strips. He explained that a kinsman who worked in a local meat-packing house had gathered up discarded scraps of plastic strapping and begun weaving them into baskets. Chia Ker Lor was so intrigued with the idea that his relative gave him an armful of the plastic for his own use.

I soon learned that over the past several years, Chia Ker Lor and other Laotian immigrants had begun to supply their communities in the United States with these sturdy, colorful, handcrafted containers. I

A sampling of Chia Ker Lor's plastic strap baskets and floor mats on display at a Philadelphia festival in 1987. Photograph by Glenn Hinson

realized I was in the presence of a dynamic, actively pursued folk artifact tradition, one characterized by, and limited to, the needs and aesthetic preferences shared by folk artists and their communities. My curiosity was about equal to, and reinforced by, the amused surprise displayed by Hmong friends and consultants when they learned that anyone could be so interested in such a mundane topic as the daily use of plastic strap baskets. I was soon to discover that this craft had attracted attention before. The 1986 Kohler Arts Center touring exhibit, "Hmong Art: Tradition and Change," for example, featured several plastic strap baskets made by a Wisconsin resident.[2] Conversations with Hmong art sponsors across the country have also revealed a growing interest in the possibility of marketing these baskets to a wider public. Yet the medium itself—plastic—challenges the popular conception of folk art. The adoption by the Hmong of polypropylene for fiber, however, is not an isolated example in the ever-changing world of traditional arts. Several researchers have recently noted the preferences of some traditional textile artists for synthetic fabrics.[3] In the public eye, such plastics are deemed the antithesis of "true" folk materials. Plastic, in fact, tends to be the very word used to describe the slick, the superficial, the inorganic, the synthetic, and the nonbiodegradable. Metaphorically—as the popular vernacular and such social commentators as filmmakers Mike Nichols (*The Graduate*) and John Waters (*Polyester*) tell us—*plastics* and *polyester* also refer to the unethical, exploitative, and heartless behaviors of modern technological man. Most Hmong do not share these biases and aversions (though they may be aware of them) but instead see something rather different in the use of this material.

What do Southeast Asian basketmakers see in the use of plastic as a weaving material? Where does the significance of these baskets lie? My interest piqued by such questions, I soon learned that handmade plastic strap baskets enjoyed popularity not only in Hmong communities in the United States but also across rural and urban Southeast Asia.

On the premise that maintenance and change in any tradition—including basketmaking—depend upon the willed actions of individuals, my investigation of this phenomena focuses primarily on the experiences, knowledge, and practices of one Hmong basketmaker, Mr. Chia Ker Lor. Telling his story properly, however, requires additional information about traditional Hmong basketmaking and its importance in communities of the past and present.

Like most Hmong men in Laos, Chia Ker Lor began learning to make baskets in his early teens. Essential to the conduct of everyday life throughout Southeast Asia and China, woven bamboo and cane is slept on, cooked with, eaten from, and played with. Baskets, by nature light and portable, contain and carry farm products, clothing, animals, water, and small children. Basket forms categorize material possessions; further, they define boundaries between the worthwhile and the useless. Winnowers separate grain from chaff; mats distinguish floor from ground. Clothes- and workbaskets protect their contents from dirt; dustpans and insect screens save the hands ceaseless labor.

In Laotian Hmong villages, it is the men who find and cut the cane and bamboo,

Above: Chia Ker Lor weaves his baskets from coils of plastic strapping, shown on the floor beside him. His floor mat and baskets are on the shelf behind him. Photograph by Glenn Hinson, 1987

Right: Three baskets owned by Wang Moua of Morganton, North Carolina. The baskets were made by Youa Kue Moua, who lives in Wisconsin. Photograph by Sally Peterson, 1988

SOME WEK
POIS

THEY WERE ESCAPING
TO THAILAND

Above: This detail from an embroidered Hmong "story cloth" is captioned "They were escaping to Thailand." The figures on the cloth mirror the experience of Chia Ker Lor and his family when they too fled Laos to Thailand, with all their worldly goods packed in baskets on their backs. Embroidery by Mrs. Youa Vang of Thailand, about 1984. Collection of Mrs. Pang Xiong Sirirathasuk. Photograph by Sally Peterson

Right: A traditional pack-basket made in Laos. Compare it with the baskets shown in the Hmong story cloth "They were escaping to Thailand." Collection of Mrs. Xee Yang, Morganton, North Carolina. Photograph by Sally Peterson

hauling it home, often over considerable distances, from the mountainous forests. And it is the men who soak, split, plait, and weave the tough fibers into basket shapes. Basketmaking remains a traditionally male occupation and is a vital contribution to domestic order. Chia Ker Lor learned this craft from watching his elders, who in turn offered cogent criticism of his first efforts. He translates his grandfather's words:

Son, you don't make it—
    if, after me, I die—
no one to show you to make.
Please, you have to learn after me.*
(Peterson, Interview, Sept. 12, 1987)

It took Chia Ker Lor more than three years to master the intricacies of basketmaking. Yet, like most young men in the Hmong community, Chia Ker Lor could produce six basket types before he was married, the six basic shapes considered essential to a

*The quotation is set as poetry in order to represent Chia Ker Lor's pattern of speech and emphasis.

competent maker's repertoire: dustpan, carrying basket, floor mat, clothing basket, latticed winnower, and insect screen.

Satisfying the family's needs for baskets aids a man's reputation for industriousness. Chia Ker Lor's son Chou Lor explains:

It's a man's job to cut bamboo.
If he wants to get married,
    he has to make his own knife,
    to cut wood.
If he's the man,
    then he's supposed to do that.
    For the lady.
If he doesn't do that,
    her friends will say she has a bad
    husband.
(Peterson, Interview, Sept. 12, 1987)

Women rarely need to learn the art of weaving bamboo. Young Chao Lor explained that a woman might learn if her son or husband was lazy; but she could just as easily ask a kinsman or clanmember to make her a basket. She would probably then cook a meal or do some other work for him in return. But, Chao insisted, they never bought baskets from each other. There was just no need for that.

In January 1976, Chia Ker Lor's family learned that hostile troops of the newly declared Republic of the Democratic Peoples

of Laos were approaching their mountain village in Sayaboury province. Fearing for their lives, they hurriedly packed their portable belongings into pack baskets and trekked over the mountains to sanctuary in Thailand. Along with tens of thousands of other escaping Laotians, the Lors took refuge in one of the many camps established by the United Nations. Refugee camps at first permitted Hmong residents to rent land in the nearby countryside; taking advantage of this policy, Chia Ker Lor supported his wife and nine children by farming during the day, returning to the camp at night. Five years later, Thai authorities revoked this privilege in an effort to curb the movement of Laotian partisans across the border, thereby restricting the Hmong to camp confines. Stripped of his traditional means of support, Chia Ker Lor seized upon basketmaking as an occupational alternative, transforming quotidian craft into commodity. Local Thai Hmong of the Lor family name brought their clan brother bamboo, which he paid for in baskets. He would make one for his suppliers, one for himself. Those that he kept were subsequently traded for food. Though baskets retained their importance as storage containers and cooking implements in the refugee camps, exchange networks shifted

Chia Ker Lor weaves a plastic strap basket in his North Philadelphia home. Photograph by Sally Peterson, 1987

Chia Ker Lor displays his "two-way weave" floor mat. Photograph by Sally Peterson, 1988

strap baskets and the materials for their making have become widespread throughout Southeast Asia. Chia Ker Lor, however, reports never seeing plastic baskets until arriving in the United States.

After six years in the refugee camp, the Lor family again packed their belongings into baskets and boxes and moved to Philadelphia, sponsored by a clan brother in the United States. But life in the United States provided few opportunities for Chia Ker Lor to support his family. Sustained largely through welfare, Mr. Lor busied himself with studying English, tending to the affairs of his clan in North Philadelphia, and looking after the younger children.

Chia Ker Lor also spent much time reproducing the tools, artifacts, and structures needed to maintain many forms of Hmong expressive culture. Exhibiting the skills of a highly inventive artisan, Mr. Lor transformed scrap wood into spirit altars, shaped broken pipes into stamps for incising spirit paper, and carved tree stumps into hat molds. He designed and constructed a quilt frame for his daughters, who sew for the flourishing quilting trade in neighboring Lancaster County. One day, at a loss for a tool to gouge out the nodes in a slender stick of bamboo, Chia Ker Lor resorted to heating the tip of a television antenna to burn through the wood, then fashioned beveled fingerholes and mouthpiece to create a flute. Into this world of inventive and persistent, indeed, stubborn craftmanship entered the gift of plastic strapping.

from exclusive dealings with clan and kin to embrace contacts throughout the camp and in local Thai markets. For Mr. Lor and many other camp residents, baskets became merchandise to be traded and sold.

Refugee camp life brought together folk from different provinces, ethnic groups, and occupations, providing increased opportunities for exchanging goods and technical knowledge—including basket designs, shapes, and uses. Former residents report that lengths of recycled plastic strips, color coordinated into bundles, were available in farmers' markets near some of the camps. Fashioning baskets from surplus plastic strapping soon became a part of many refugees' technical repertoires. Indeed, plastic

Without access to inexpensively marketed plastic strapping in the United States, most Hmong plastic basketmakers must salvage their supplies from workplace waste. One Pennsylvania craftswoman pays her supervisor two dollars for every bunch of plastic he gathers from the factory floor and sets aside for her. Each bundle yields two or three large baskets, which she can then sell for thirty-five dollars a piece. Hmong who work in North Carolina textile mills gather plastic remnants left over

The design of this basket by Chia Ker Lor is called "Going to Meet a Friend." Photograph by Sally Peterson, 1988

from binding boxes of socks. When Chia Ker Lor's cousin (and supplier) moved to Wisconsin, a local Philadelphia butcher helped us to locate a plastics corporation that donated coils of strapping that had not measured up to specifications. Both means of acquisition—by salvage or donation—limit basket design possibilities, forcing basketmakers to make do with what colors, quantities, widths, and thicknesses they find.

Chia Ker Lor says that he has grown to like working with plastic, particularly now that his fingertips have adjusted to the additional strain caused by the material's slipperiness. When he first began his experiments with the strapping, Mr. Lor anchored every three rows with loops of copper wire, twisting the ends into a tight knot. He later improved upon this method by repeatedly splitting the strapping; he uses the thin strips to weave binding rows at the basket bases and rims. This technique enables him to maintain both an even tension and a tight, secure weave.

Mr. Lor uses two weaving patterns to make baskets. He translates one of these as the "one-way weave"—a basic tabby weave of "one over, one under." This simple, repetitive design makes the strongest basket; when using quarter inch or smaller strapping, it is also one of the most difficult weaves to execute. The close-set, interlocking pattern requires nimble fingers, and the plastic's brittle edges chafe the skin. Chia Ker Lor's more complex "two-way weave" is a quill pattern that produces diagonals. When using three colors, Mr. Lor weaves the strips into a houndstooth design; when using two colors, he often adds visual interest by repeating one step in the design sequence at the basket's half-way point. This move reverses the direction of the diagonals, leaving a V-shaped intersection. He calls the resulting design "Going to Meet a Friend."

Though admitting that plastic cannot be used for some basket forms he would like to make (any latticed or open weave is difficult to reproduce with plastic), Chia Ker Lor says he would rather not return to bamboo solely. Plastic does not split when you don't want it to; nor does it need to be soaked. Picking up strapping at a local factory is much easier than locating, cutting, and hauling loads of bamboo—and it does not require as much storage space. Most importantly, unlike natural, organic fibers, plastic comes in colors—deeply saturated, intense colors that remind him of the vibrant hues traditional to Hmong needlework. Chia Ker Lor enjoys planning the colors in his baskets; by varying color, width, and weave, he can create optical effects reminiscent of the maze patterns appliqued by Hmong women. Like these needleworkers, he prefers bright color contrasts, balanced by additions of complementary hues. Unfortunately, he sighs, his choice of color is limited to the dye lots chosen by the plastics industry; he is pining for red.

Chia Ker Lor both gives and sells his baskets within the local Hmong community, with the exchanges generally following kin and clan linkages. Other makers in other communities distribute their woven creations in the same way. The plastic baskets I have seen used by Hmong in Pennsylvania, California, Michigan, Washington, and North Carolina serve many of the same purposes as their bamboo models. Families use them to collect and to store garden produce, to hold utensils, to pack food to take to the New Year celebration. A mother

stores her baby's clothes in a basket; a factory worker uses one as a purse; a teenager keeps one to hold her boyfriend's letters. Many women use them as sewing baskets, and several needle artists employ large, capacious baskets for storing and transporting the intricate needlework they sell at craft fairs and folk festivals. Plastic strap baskets provide easy access to their contents; they are easy to move from place to place; they make it simple to find what you're looking for. They help to order life in an accustomed way, a way familiar from the years before their arrival in America. The plastic is extremely durable; it doesn't rip, fade, mildew, or peel. It withstands extremes in temperatures and can be washed endlessly. And it is considered pretty, particularly in the color combinations created by the basketmakers. Knowing the craftsperson makes it easy to request changes in shape, size, and color. Cheaper plastic containers can be bought at the local K-Mart, but experience has taught consumers that the quality of handcrafted items is superior to machine-made goods, and they know they can trust the workmanship of a Hmong basketmaker.

Although the general purposes of baskets have not changed radically, their public contexts and much of their contents have. As a result, few contemporary basket shapes replicate the most common Laotian forms. A packbasket strapped to the back would make some work easier, but Hmong consumers prefer inconspicuous shapes that blend easily into the American urban landscape. Most baskets, now smaller than their Laotian counterparts, usually sport two carrying handles.

Chia Ker Lor may differ from other basketmakers in that he is willing to produce baskets not specifically designed to fill a contemporary need of family or community. The sheer quantity of plastic donated by the local plastics factory—and his leisure time—have enabled Mr. Lor to experiment with translating the full range of his basket repertoire into a plastic medium. For months after the initial donation, each time I visited Chia Ker Lor, he would disappear into the basement and reappear with a new creation. He has reproduced rice winnowers, floor mats, arrow sheaths, and even the clothesbasket his mother-in-law gave his wife on their wedding day. His nephew now comes to him for plastic strips, and together they are working on developing colorful steamers for sticky rice, woven from plastic.

Chia Ker Lor doubts that the local Hmong community will display much interest in owning his newer, labor-intensive creations. No one needs a rice winnower anymore; the mats are hard to clean and expensive. Perhaps he will sell them to Americans, he says, or someday donate them to a museum. He doesn't use them himself.

Mr. Lor's efforts to market his creations outside of the Hmong community have met with little success. A neighborhood Asian market sells a few for him, mainly to other Asian immigrant customers. His vibrant patterns and dextrous demonstrations have attracted attention at craft fairs, but most fairgoers politely finger the plastic and shake their heads, unwilling to pay handicraft prices for the bright plastic. Most plastic strap baskets made by the Hmong seem destined to remain within their communities—an anomaly in the high-demand market of authentic folk art.

In all my discussions with owners of plastic strap baskets and in all my observations of their homes, I have never heard or seen any indication that these containers are consciously stressed as markers of ethnicity.

In this recent clothes basket (left), Chia Ker Lor has used the traditional design brought from his Laotian homeland (as shown right). Photograph by Sally Peterson, 1987

They act neither as nostalgic reminders of the homeland nor as deliberate expressions of an articulated Hmong aesthetic, unlike the highly valued but infrequently used needlework. The baskets are in the homes to do work, and they stay in the homes because they do that work predictably, efficiently, and attractively. But perhaps a deeper meaning can be deduced—a meaning that precludes look, feel, or function, a meaning that reaches back to the process itself. Meaning adheres to particular ways of doing things, creating a mystique of motive and method that evokes deeply felt responses among members of a group. Such an "affecting process" prevails throughout the business of living in Hmong culture, and plastic strap baskets are but one of many catalysts for its enactment.[4] The process operates in the arena of social relations, its philosophy arises from self-reliance, while its praxis depends upon networks of clan and kin. Within this closely knit social structure, traditional—or innovative—ideas that enhance the quality of life are most readily accepted if proffered by clan members. Such ideas must offer both practical solutions to problems and strengthen cross-community ties. I believe this assumption applies equally well to matters on a material, spiritual, medical, or juridical plane. Indeed, the stresses upon this process arising from confrontations with American culture cause great concern in Hmong communities. In the case of plastic strap baskets, function, technical mastery, and aesthetic compliance are all integral to the craft's popularity. But these factors are not the locus of the baskets' meaning. That meaning lies in the union of utility—which enables self-reliance—with the source, which is Hmong.

The individual, creative spark that inspires Chia Ker Lor to invent, adapt, and innovate helps maintain his personal sense of integrity, allowing him to simultaneously serve his family, his clan, his self, and his ancestral spirits. Some of his creations are useful to his community, others are useful to himself alone, but all become references, resources for the next project. The volatile combination of personal creativity and traditional process has received community sanction before, and will again.

I once saw a bumper sticker on a Hmong-owned car in Philadelphia that stated well the spirit of self-reliance and responsibility Chia Ker Lor enacts: "Hmoob Yuav Tsum Hlub Hmoob"—"The Hmong must care for the Hmong."

NOTES

1. A version of this paper was presented at the 1987 meetings of the American Folklore Society in Albuquerque, New Mexico. For their gracious hospitality and kind words, I would like to thank Chia Ker Lor and his family, Pang Xiong Sirirathasuk, Bao Yang, Xee Yang, Wang Seng Khang, and Cha Yang. Many thanks to Glenn Hinson for his insightful comments.

2. *See* Joanne Cubbs, ed., *Hmong Art: Tradition and Change* (Sheboygan, Wisconsin: John Michael Kohler Arts Center, 1986), 131,133.

3. *See,* for example, Geraldine N. Johnson, "More for Warmth than for Looks: Quilts of the Blue Ridge Mountains." In *Pieced by Mother,* edited by Jeannette Lasansky (Lewisburg, Pa: Oral Traditions Project, 1988), 50.

4. In proposing the term "affecting process," I am borrowing heavily from the theories of Robert Plant Armstrong, whose efforts to delineate the emotive experience of cultural systems of art first appear in *The Affecting Presence* (Urbana, Illinois: University of Illinois Press, 1972).

"Bulrush Is Silver, Sweetgrass Is Gold"

The Enduring Art of Sea Grass Basketry

BY DALE ROSENGARTEN

Mary Vanderhorst sews a sweetgrass basket in the small shed behind her roadside stand on Highway 17, Mt. Pleasant, South Carolina. Photograph by David A. Taylor, March 1987

On the afternoon of March 25, 1988, about thirty people gathered in front of The Charleston Museum, under the hot sun of the early South Carolina spring. We were a mixed bunch—basketmakers and botanists, folklorists and environmentalists, photographers and journalists—about to embark on a field trip in search of sweetgrass (*Muhlenbergia filipes* or *M. capillaris*), a long-stemmed grass uniquely suited to the making of coiled baskets. Once accessible along the seacoast from North Carolina to Florida but now diminished or put off-limits by real estate development, sweetgrass is in short supply.

Our destination was Seabrook Island, a scenic barrier island twenty-three miles southwest of Charleston, maintained as a private residential and resort community. We were escorted through the gate by a member of the Seabrook Natural History Group. As we drove past substantial modern houses, discretely placed and well weathered, a ripple of excitement passed through the basketmakers in the party. To those of us who were seeing sweetgrass for the first time, they pointed out lush tufts of *Muhlenbergia* growing on road medians and in landscaped yards, next to the more predictable pampas grass, palmetto, and yucca.

The excitement caught everyone. We were like a group of bird-watchers who had just sighted a Bachman's warbler, that rare songbird once local to the area. We parked near a clubhouse and a cluster of new condominiums. Several more members of the Natural History Group joined us. We crossed a boardwalk onto the beach and walked east towards the neighboring island of Kiawah. In troughs behind the first line of dunes lay acres and acres of sweetgrass growing in the shade of myrtles.

Sea grass basketry is an African art form that has been practiced continuously in South Carolina for three hundred years. Wherever rice was grown on the South Atlantic coast, coiled baskets were made to be used in the harvest. During the long decline of rice production—from the Civil War to World War I—Afro-American basketmakers continued to "sew" baskets on reconstructed plantations and on the small, family farms they had acquired.

All the basket shapes from this era may be seen today on basket stands along Highway 17 North and on street corners in Charleston. Materials, functions, and techniques of construction have changed, however. Sweetgrass sewn with palmetto leaf has replaced bulrush bound with oak splits or palmetto butt as the preferred materials in the baskets. The wide winnowing trays called "fanners," which once served to separate the chaff from rice, now might hold magazines or be hung on the wall. A century ago, vegetable baskets, balanced deftly on the head, carried mountains of produce to market. Big, open baskets still are made, but for indoor uses. Covered storage baskets, in the plantation era, might have contained grain or yarn or sewing supplies. The grain they once held is long gone, but sewing and yarn baskets remain staples of the trade.

Today, lowcountry basketry is concentrated in the community of Mt. Pleasant,

across the Cooper River from Charleston. Fifty years ago Mt. Pleasant was a quiet village, surrounded by farm settlements. Now it is a burgeoning suburb, busily swallowing farms and woodlots, and turning country lanes into highways. The generation of basketmakers currently approaching middle age grew up in this period of change. Daughters and granddaughters of farm women, they have adapted to a faster pace of life and a money economy, working in hospitals, restaurants, hotels, or schools, driving automobiles, buying food in supermarkets. In effect they have traveled from country to city without having moved at all.

Since the New South has arrived with a vengeance, the baskets and their makers are caught in a paradox of "sun belt" development: tourists and new residents certainly help basket sales, but the resorts and subdivisions built to accommodate the newcomers often destroy or cut off access to the basketmakers' prime raw material—sweetgrass.

Yet what is remarkable about the tradition of lowcountry basketry is not the current threats to its well-being but the fact that it has survived so long. Coiled sea grass basketry is a tree with two branches. Work baskets made for outdoor uses were dominant in the plantation era; today they are

collectors' items and museum pieces. Household baskets, which constituted the lesser branch in the nineteenth century, now dominate the scene.

The division of baskets by function has antecedents in Africa, where granaries, fences, reed work, thatching, traps, and heavy field baskets tended to be made by men, while mats, smaller baskets for storing and serving food, and fancy baskets were made by women for household use. On lowcountry plantations, basketmaking was usually reported to have been men's work. Plantation "handicraftsmen," wrote David Doar, recalling life on the Santee River before the Civil War, "made all the baskets (out of river rushes cured and sewed with white oak strips) that were used on the place." Constructed of durable fibers, work baskets were designed to withstand years of hard labor. They were bound with an interlocking stitch, the binders of one row passing under the stitches of the row before. Collecting materials might occupy a few "hands" for several days, usually late in the summer; making baskets might take two or three weeks. Fanners were by far the most common form. Once threshing and winnowing began, overseers would issue fanners by the dozen and the whole plantation work force would turn to the task.

Right: Fanning rice at Wedgefield Plantation, about 1890. Photograph courtesy of the Rice Museum, Georgetown, South Carolina

Below: A customer looks over the wares offered for sale by Annabell Ellis and Florence Frazier on Kiawah Island, South Carolina, June 1986. The real estate sign to the right speaks of the dilemma for lowcountry basketmakers, who welcome tourists and newcomers to the area but fear that overdevelopment will destroy traditional ways of life. Photograph by Dale Rosengarten, courtesy of the McKissick Museum

Household baskets, made of finer elements, belonged to the domestic sphere and were more "on the woman's side." Doar described, for example, "small baskets with handles which the women used, and out of a finer kind of grass, sewed with palmetto or oak strip, a very neat sewing-basket, some of them three-storied; that is, one on top of the other, each resting on the cover of the one below and getting smaller as they went up." Modern sweetgrass baskets are direct descendants of these household styles. Indeed, two- and three-tiered sewing baskets still are made, on request, by Mt. Pleasant basketmakers of the older generation.

The image of the "Vegetable Woman," her "head tote" basket heaped with produce, was used to lure tourists to Charleston. Photograph by G. W. Johnson, about 1900. Courtesy of the Carolina Art Association/Gibbes Museum of Art

Double basket by Mary Jane Manigault. Photograph by Will Barnes, 1987, courtesy of the McKissick Museum

Though strictly a country craft, sea grass baskets have been part of the cityscape since antebellum times. From black settlements around Charleston and Savannah, first slaves and later freedmen and women carried produce and other marketable items to the city to sell. Traveling by ox-cart and ferry, vendors toted fish and shellfish in sacks or split oak baskets; vegetables, as a rule, were transported in coiled rush baskets on the head.

So striking was the phenomenon of the street vendor bearing a "head tote" basket that, by 1900, the image was widely used to lure tourists to Charleston. George W. Johnson, who ran an umbrella shop on Hasell Street and indulged a passion for photography, immortalized numerous street vendors with his camera. "One of the most interesting sights of Charleston," touted the caption of a turn-of-the-century postcard, "is the negro vegetable vender." On the streets of the city, visitors could see market people "of both sexes and of all ages . . . bearing on their heads enormous round baskets of produce," and hear them "singing their wares in quaint dialect cries that sound to the unfamiliar ear like utterances of a foreign race." At a time when wealthy Americans were discovering the pleasures of watering holes in the Caribbean and pueblos in the Spanish Southwest,

Ox carts carried produce and other goods from black settlements into the market cities of Charleston and Savannah. Photograph by G. W. Johnson, St. Andrew's Parish, about 1900. Courtesy of Carolina Art Association/Gibbes Museum of Art

Charleston promoters were boasting that their city had exotic people, too.

But this image did not please everyone. When the South Carolina Interstate and West Indian Exposition of 1901 unveiled a statue in front of the "Negro Building," educated blacks—"the so-called 'new' negroes of Charleston"—protested that the work represented "the Negro in too menial guise." The sculpture was designed by Charles Albert Lopez, a Mexican-American artist living in New York. It depicted a muscular figure, modeled on Booker T. Washington, chief commissioner of the exposition's Negro Department, with one hand on an anvil and the other on a plough, a hammer and a hoe resting at his feet. A young man with a leather apron and the tools of a mechanic sat strumming a banjo. The crowning symbol of the romantic group was a stately black woman, her chin held high, balancing a basket on top of her head.

Art historians may recognize in the "Negro Group" the noble peasant of late-nineteenth-century European sculpture. But to Charleston's black elite, glorification of the tillers of the soil threatened to undermine the progress of the race. During slavery, "free people of color" had congregated in cities and defended their margin of liberty by distancing themselves from plantation slaves. At the turn of the century, they still were intent on defining themselves in terms of morals, education, and industrial activities, and not in terms of manual labor.

Early in this century, a community of black farm families in Christ Church Parish began mass-producing and selling "show baskets" made of sweetgrass. Adorned with longleaf pine needles and sewn with strips of palmetto leaf, sweetgrass baskets became a Mt. Pleasant specialty. As basketmakers pursued new markets, styles and decorative motifs proliferated and women came to dominate the craft.

An activity that under slavery gave men a measure of independence, under freedom offered economic opportunities and avenues of expression for women. Adapting traditional forms and inventing new ones, sewers developed a large repertory of functional shapes—bread trays, table mats, flower and fruit baskets, shopping bags, hat box baskets, missionary bags, clothes hampers, sewing, crochet, and knitting baskets, spittoon baskets, wall pockets, picnic baskets, thermos bottles or wine coolers, ring trays, cord baskets, cake baskets, wastepaper baskets, and platters in the shape of small fanners. Made in Mt. Pleasant, the baskets found their first major market in Charleston. The city's proximity was critical to the survival of the craft; even today, the sweetgrass basket is commonly known as the "Charleston basket."

In 1916, a young Charleston merchant named Clarence W. Legerton initiated a wholesale trade in baskets. Early advertising copy for the Sea Grass Basket Company describes the "pleasing and artistic" contrast "between the white strips of palmetto and the sage green grass." It stresses the limitations of production—the restricted range and season of sweetgrass and "the

small number of negroes making strictly first grade baskets"—and claims that for several years "the output has been absorbed by local gift shops for sale to tourists and visitors." "Owing to the shortage of foreign made baskets"—presumably because of World War I—sweetgrass baskets were being offered "for the first time in quantity" and were finding "a ready market."

Legerton is remembered today among basketmakers as "Mr. Leviston" or "Mr. Lester." They tell how he would come every other Saturday to Sam Coakley's house at Hamlin Beach, where the sewers would have gathered with their baskets. He would examine each basket "thoroughly all over" and "bang on it with his knuckles." He could tell by the sound if it was "well-made." "My mother used to make the basket and box them up and bag them up and take them over there," recalls basketmaker Louise White, "and he'll go through and he'll get what he wants and he'll box them up and ship them away."

Legerton bought large quantities of baskets and sold them in his bookstore on King Street and through his catalog business, called Seagrassco. In the years for which we have accounts, the company's biggest

Seagrassco catalog, about 1920. Courtesy of Clifford L. Legerton, North Charleston, South Carolina

The "Negro Group," designed by Charles Albert Lopez for the South Carolina Interstate and West Indian Exposition, 1902. The romantic depiction, which recalls the noble peasant of late-nineteenth-century European sculpture, did not appeal to many of Charleston's black elite. Photograph by G. W. Johnson. Courtesy of the Carolina Art Association/Gibbes Museum of Art

monthly expenditure occurred in August 1918, when Legerton paid $1,238.89 for baskets. (More typical monthly figures ranged from a few dollars to several hundred dollars.) In a farm community where people produced most of what they consumed, $1,200 would have gone a long way, even divided as it must have been among many families.

With Legerton in the picture, baskets were the new cash crop. He continued to buy baskets from Mt. Pleasant sewers for more than thirty years and, according to his second son, "tried his level best to get them to organize to mass produce." He paid very little for each piece; in those days "a whole sheet" of baskets (as many as would fit on a bedsheet) cost him $12. Marking the price

Viola Jefferson in front of a basket stand, September 1938. The sign reads "Stop and Buy Baskets Made by Cld. People of S.C." Photograph by Bluford Muir. Courtesy of Francis Marion National Forest, McClellanville, South Carolina

up 50 to 100 percent, Legerton & Co. could still sell wholesale. Buyers in New York or the Midwest, for example, could acquire a dozen five-inch sewing baskets for $4.25.

By 1930, the basketmakers had developed a strategy for selling directly to tourists. Traffic along Highway 17 increased perceptibly through the 1920s, as Florida experienced its first residential boom. Northerners who didn't like cold winters and had money to spend drove south to the new "frontier." The paving of Highway 17 and the construction of the Cooper River Bridge turned the coastal route that passes through Mt. Pleasant into an efficient north-south artery. Basketsewers began displaying their wares on the road and the basket stand was born.

The first basket stands were nothing more than a chair or overturned box placed on the edge of the road. Stands quickly evolved into a novel architectural form consisting of posts or saplings set upright in the ground, with strips of scrap wood nailed horizontally between them, sheltered by a roof of burlap or tin. Nails served as pegs for hanging baskets. Generally constructed by men, basket stands became a place where women and children congregated. Sheds built behind the stands and outfitted with stoves, beds, and chairs provided some comforts for the basket sellers.

Betsy Johnson is reputed to have had the first "basket house" on the highway in front of her home. She and her daughter, Edna Rouse, would hang a few baskets from wooden "arms" nailed to a shed, to advertise their merchandise. By the 1940s, Mrs. Johnson was commissioning work from numbers of people to fill "big orders" and sending "great boxes" of baskets away.

In the history of the marketing of baskets, the stands were a great advance. They showed the work to good advantage, gave the makers some visibility, and most important, allowed them to eliminate the middleman and charge the retail price for their baskets. "I set up a stand back when there weren't hardly any stands on the highway," recalled the late Irene Foreman. "Me and Hessie Huger set up a stand in 'Four-

Mary Vanderhorst's basket stand, shared with her sister and a friend, is typical of the stands along Highway 17 in Mt. Pleasant, South Carolina. Photograph by David A. Taylor, March 1987

Mile'"—neighborhoods in Mt. Pleasant are named for their distance from Charleston. "We figure we could make a whole lot more money than just sewing for Mr. Leviston. He'd pay twenty cents for a twelve-inch piece. If you sell them yourself you can get double that, all of fifty and seventy-five cents for a basket."

The stands also freed basketsewers from the constraints of commission work, which called for specific quantities of a limited number of styles. "You can make your basket the way you want and you can make 'em the price you want," says Evelyina Foreman, who as a youngster sewed for Legerton, as her mother had before her.

By 1949, thirty-one stands, selling chiefly to tourists, were counted along a two-mile stretch of Highway 17 in the vicinity of Christ Church. "Gleaming . . . automobiles" would pull up in front of the stands, reported the *News and Courier*'s Jack Leland, appreciating the irony. "Persons from the large and modern centers of this country's industrial areas" would stop to look at "an importation of the artistry of African workers." A photograph of "Betsy's Basket Shop" accompanied Leland's article, showing Mrs. Johnson beside a display of hat box baskets, wall pockets, trash baskets, fruit and flower baskets, shopping bags, and table mats.

While the through-traffic trade provided a reliable market for sweetgrass baskets, efforts to merchandise old-style work baskets met with less success. In some cases, the problem was the distance from markets. In others, it was the loss of functions for work baskets, or the diminishing number of makers, as the agricultural economy of the lowcountry declined.

The Penn School had been established in 1862 on St. Helena Island, a remote sea island east of Beaufort. An abolitionist enterprise initially supported by northern relief agencies, Penn soon became the leading educational resource of the black farm community. When the school was reorganized in 1904 after the "industrial" pattern of Virginia's Hampton Institute, "Native Island Basketry" was added to the curriculum. Penn's directors were trying to make island life more viable by teaching practical skills in both farming and manual arts. A cash incentive was offered from the start. "There is a real commercial demand for these native island baskets," noted Penn's *Annual Report* of 1910. For the next thirty-five years, Penn sold baskets made in the school's shop and in homes across St.

Helena. Penn bought baskets outright, paying "cash direct to the basketmakers," after deducting 10 percent of the selling price for handling.

In 1924, Penn's *Annual Report* claimed that the demand for baskets "has been steadily increasing"—that year 148 baskets and 24 corn-shuck mats were sold. List prices for eight styles of bulrush baskets sewn with palmetto butt ranged from $2.00 for a sewing basket to $12.50 for a large clothes hamper, plus transportation charges. Corn shuck door mats sold for eighty cents apiece. The main markets for St. Helena baskets most likely were Philadelphia, Boston, and other faraway cities where Penn's benefactors lived. While the demand may have been increasing, the income from basket sales was not sufficient to inspire young students.

As enrollment in the basketmaking class declined, the usually upbeat *Annual Report* expressed alarm lest Native Island Basketry "be allowed to become a lost art. This will happen," warned the 1928 *Report*, "unless Penn School can keep this shop open and interest the younger generation in it." On the eve of the Depression, basketry definitely was losing ground. Boys who in years past would have taken to the work no longer were willing to invest so many hours for such meager return. "I couldn't see no sense in it," says Leroy Browne, whose father taught the class for thirty-four years. "I spent six months in the basket shop and made half a basket." In light of the prices baskets were bringing, young people generally preferred to do something else. "In this age of machines and speed," Penn's administrators confessed, basketmaking was "slow and tedious work." Baskets themselves might be growing in "worth and popularity," but the kind of labor it took to make them was falling out of favor.

During slavery, on St. Helena as on other sea islands, rice was grown not commercially but as a provision crop, for home consumption. Here it was the dietary preferences of the slaves, rather than the profit motives of the masters, which determined whether coiled baskets would be made. Basketmaking persisted well into the twentieth century thanks to the Penn School's efforts to preserve the craft. Besides the promise of financial return, cultural motives always had played a part in Penn's venture. "This industry was brought from Africa in the early slave days," declared the *Annual Report* of 1910. It belongs "as truly to the Negro as the Indian basket belongs to the Indian." But by 1950, Penn's curriculum had become obsolete; sentiment alone could not keep Native Island Basketry alive.

One hundred fifty miles north of St. Helena—sixty miles up Highway 17 from Mt. Pleasant—another effort to merchandise lowcountry baskets was underway. On Waccamaw Neck, in the richest section of the old rice kingdom, the Pawley's Island Hammock Shop opened its doors in 1938. The shop's first brochure advertised a unique array of coiled basketry: old-time work baskets made of "bull rush bound with oak" were displayed side by side with Mt. Pleasant styles in sweetgrass and pine.

Recognizing both branches of the sea grass tradition, the brochure described rush baskets as a thing of the past, while it applauded the artistic innovations, "such as ingenious pine needle trim," of the sweetgrass forms. Welcome Beese, who had been born in slavery on Oatland Plantation, demonstrated bulrush basketmaking outside the shop. More than a hundred years old, he was pictured sitting next to an old mortar and pestle, against which were propped seven rush baskets. "The rice fanner, reminiscent of the good old days 'befo' de wa', will be relegated to the lost arts," predicted the brochure. "'Uncle Beese' sits . . . patiently weaving and, no doubt, meditates upon 'dese changeful times.'"

Besides nostalgia for the glory days of the rice plantation, the Hammock Shop's promotion of rush baskets expressed a new curiosity about African art. "An old white hunter," veteran of big game hunts in Africa, asserted that Afro-American baskets closely resembled in design and workmanship, "those made by certain tribes today." Looking at the Hammock Shop's baskets, he claimed to be able to identify "from which of these ancestral tribes some of the Carolina descendants had sprung."

The shop's range of sweetgrass styles was similar to Seagrassco's earlier selection, suggesting that basket forms were rather stable through the 1930s. At $1.50, a "Cocktail Tray" containing seven coasters was the top of the Mt. Pleasant line. Rush baskets were comparably priced; waste baskets, fanners, and deep fanners sold for $1.00, $1.25, and $2.00, respectively. Fifty years later, the greatly expanded Hammock Shop continues to carry Mt. Pleasant baskets, while traditional rush basketry in Georgetown County indeed has been "relegated to the lost arts."

The same year the Hammock Shop opened, the Charleston Chamber of Commerce published a pamphlet entitled "An Art as Old as Africa," promoting "Handmade Basketry, the Art of South Carolina Negroes" as indigenous to "America's Most Historic City." Following two pages of text, the pamphlet lists twelve styles of baskets, illustrated with photographs, which could be ordered from the "Distributing Office" on Meeting Street. There is a curious discrepancy between the text, which consistently refers to *rush* baskets, and the photographs, which clearly show sweetgrass forms decorated with pine straw. While pointing out the transition

Right: Jannie Cohen with a bundle of bulrush, Hilton Head, South Carolina, March 1986. Although not as flexible as sweetgrass, bulrush is a sturdy and abundant material that allows basketmakers to produce large sculptural forms. Photograph by Ted Wathen

Below: Allen Green, Sapelo Island, Georgia, August 1985. Widely known as the last Georgians still making coiled-grass baskets, Green and his wife sell their work every summer at a crafts fair on St. Simons Island. Photograph by Dale Rosengarten. Courtesy of the McKissick Museum

from "useful but not artistic" old-style baskets to the "more artistic designs and patterns" of contemporary work, the writer evidently had not caught on that the basket materials had changed, too.

Rush basketry had not been entirely abandoned near Charleston. "Down on Edisto Island live a few old Negroes who make baskets in their spare time," reported the Works Project Administration around 1940. "Here, strange to say, the weavers are mostly men." Again, the outside observers had not understood the traditional sexual division of labor: men made rush work baskets and women made sweetgrass show baskets. The Edisto basketsewers did not "go in for fancy design, either in color or shape," but were "content to make sturdy containers which may last a family over two generations."

Except in rare instances where basketmakers have been able to tap the collectors' market, old-style work baskets have passed out of production. "When I came along," says Allen Green, who was born on Sapelo Island, Georgia, in 1907, "boys and girls could make these baskets. Plenty could make it, but all die out. I'm the only one living so far." Green and his wife sell their work at a crafts fair on St. Simons Island every summer. Widely known as the last Georgians practicing the craft, they have a hard time keeping up with the demand.

Caesar Johnson, of Hilton Head, learned to make baskets as a "tiny boy," around 1880. Seventy years later, his modest fame drew "many of the crafts-minded to his cabin." He also sold baskets through shops on Hilton Head, concentrating on four styles that proved most popular. Johnson lamented the passing of the art, explaining to a reporter in 1960 that "today's Negroes make more money at jobs" and don't want to practice a skill "that marks them as 'backwoods' or 'country.'" Johnson might be surprised to know the prices "Caesar baskets" bring in antique shops in Savannah these days.

Twenty-five years ago, at least two Hilton Head women—Beaulah Kellerson and Jannie Cohen—were selling bulrush and palmetto butt baskets on road stands along Highway 278. Mrs. Kellerson, now living in a nursing home on the island, displayed her baskets on the family's vegetable stand from the mid-fifties into the sixties. Her nephew, Abe Grant, recalls that in 1961 she was offering her big baskets for five dollars apiece. He advised her to double her prices, and he doubled the size of her display space.

Jannie Cohen was taught basketmaking by her father, Ed Green. In the 1950s she, like Mrs. Kellerson, sold her baskets on the road—round ones, "egg-shell" or oblong ones, fanners, and trash baskets. She would nail a basket to a roadside sign that announced, "Baskets for sale." She remembers selling her fanners, each the size of a dishpan with three rows built up for sides, for three dollars. Discouraged by the low prices she was getting, she quit sewing baskets but resumed in the autumn of 1985

Right top: Joseph Foreman pulling sweetgrass, April 1985. Photograph by Dale Rosengarten, courtesy of the McKissick Museum

Right bottom: Mary Jackson cutting rush, December 1984. Photograph by John McWilliams

Basket stand on Highway 17 North, Mt. Pleasant, South Carolina. The realtor's sign is ominous, as many stands are being crowded out by new shopping malls, office complexes, and residential subdivisions. Photograph by John Michael Vlach

when she was persuaded to make one for exhibition. Since then she has gone back into more or less full-time production, selling her work from her home and at the Red Piano gallery on the island. Today Mrs. Cohen is the only South Carolinian sewing old-style work baskets—sturdy, thick-coiled forms identical in shape, materials, and construction to the earliest examples of Afro-American sea grass basketry.

Some folk arts die because they lose their functions, lose their markets, or because the community that produces them is displaced or assimilated into the mainstream culture. The inventiveness and spiritual strength of the Mt. Pleasant basketmakers might not have been enough to save the lowcountry basket. If there had been no market for their work, they might have stopped sewing. Mt. Pleasant's strategic location on the main road into Charleston made it possible for basketmakers to become independent entrepreneurs, to control both the production and the marketing of their baskets. "We did the baskets with joy and with creativity, with self-pride,"

basketmaker Louise Frasier recently declared, "knowing that we can earn a living on our own with our own craft, with our own creativity, with our own inheritance." The emphasis here is on "our own"—on the community's sense of identity and self-reliance. "Mt. Pleasant is one of the only places in the United States," Mrs. Frasier believes, where people have been able "to maintain their own living and not have to depend on other people for their wages."

The irony of the basket's persistence is that it reflects a reality of dismal alternatives. Until recently, the only jobs available to black women in the lowcountry were poorly paid and menial, jobs described in the Mt. Pleasant community as "hard work," "working out," or "working for nothing." Though the income from basketmaking may be marginal, sewers enjoy an autonomy that is rare in today's working world; they can weave and sell when they want to, exercise their imagination and judgment, and work with family members in a collective enterprise.

Other incentives, too, have come into play. While sewers frequently complain that people do not want to pay what a basket is worth, basketmakers as a group have achieved a new status. "I think the biggest change," Jannie Gourdine told a Charleston journalist in 1980, "is that people look at us as artists now instead of just basket weavers." This belated public acclaim has attracted sophisticated, well-educated women back to the craft. Moved by the long, proud history of lowcountry basketry, they have become articulate exponents of the tradition.

The demand for baskets has never been greater. A small, national collector's market underwrites the trend toward artistic recognition and higher prices. Charleston's tourist traffic shows no sign of let-up, and the convention trade is just getting started. But economic expansion is a mixed blessing. A vital outlet for Mt. Pleasant baskets—the stands on Highway 17—is being crowded out by shopping malls, office complexes, and condominiums, as the city outgrows its limits. Billboards and realtors' signs form an ominous backdrop to many basket stands.

Another consequence of coastal development is the sweetgrass shortage. "Men folk"—fathers, brothers, husbands, nephews, and sons of the basketmakers—travel as far as Georgia or northern Florida to gather the grass. The costs of these trips are borne by the sewers, who have to plan for a major outlay of capital at the end of each summer, when they must stockpile enough grass to last until the gathering season begins in the spring.

The problem has been around a long time. In 1971, South Carolina ETV produced a film entitled "Gullah Baskets," documenting the African origins of the art and identifying the dwindling supply of sweetgrass as the major threat to its survival. At the same time, in Mt. Pleasant, two young anthropologists were lobbying for basketmakers to be permitted to "pull" sweetgrass in Charleston County parks.

At this critical juncture, the basketmakers again found a way to make a virtue of necessity. They reached back into their tradition and rediscovered rush. Without forethought or fanfare, they began using it in conjunction with sweetgrass around 1970. Perhaps half the baskets made today incorporate some amount of rush.

While bulrush has enabled sewers to "stretch" the sweetgrass supply, it has not replaced the finer, more flexible grass. Not everyone is willing or able to use rush. Binding rows of bulrush tightly requires strength and agility and is hard on the hands. Combining rush and sweetgrass in the same basket is an innovation not all old-timers will accept, though even purists begin their rush baskets with sweetgrass or pine needles. The fact is, bulrush cannot do everything sweetgrass can do. It is difficult to tie in a knot. It is too coarse to use in small baskets or to work into delicate decorative details.

Still, rush has its advantages. Thicker and more rigid than sweetgrass, bulrush encourages basketmakers to work on a grand scale, to make large fanners, market baskets, and hampers reminiscent of old-style work baskets. "I really love the large one now even more than I like the small one," says basketmaker Marie Manigault, "because the large one show up prettier."

The use of rush recalls the Biblical story of Moses, an association that dates from the plantation era. A religious song from the rice fields along the Combahee River, for example, included the lines:

Moses in de bull-rushes fas' asleep
Playing possum in de two bushel basket!

Though the song has disappeared, the image it evokes is very much alive. Talk to any contemporary basketmaker about bulrush and before long you will hear how the baby Moses was saved by the Pharaoh's daughter. Mary Jackson, whose work is unmistakably modern yet intensely traditional, has titled her deep, open, oblong, cross-handled basket the "Moses Basket."

Rush can be used to reinforce handles, feet, rims, and other points of stress where a basket might break. It is hollow, hence light in weight. It turns a rich, tawny brown when dried in the sun. Above all it is abundant. In the coin of the basketmaker's realm, as Henrietta Snype is fond of saying, bulrush is silver, sweetgrass is gold.

The intrinsic rewards of the craft have been enhanced since the 1970s by an expanding public interest in Afro-American folk art. In the search for the roots of black Americans, sea grass basketry provides tangible evidence of the African heritage. A cross-fertilization between African and Afro-American art is now taking place. Influenced by exposure to African basketry, either through books and exhibitions or through examples of tribal crafts brought home by family members traveling abroad, Mt. Pleasant basketmakers consciously imitate African designs. With their conical covers and big-bellied shapes, modern Mt. Pleasant baskets appear more African than earlier forms.

Coiled baskets appeal today to a broad audience, from souvenir hunters to art collectors, from housewives who want a bread basket to set on the table to museum curators who want to document and exhibit the craft and preserve examples in dust-free, climate-controlled cabinets. Prices have risen dramatically over the past two decades, doubling every five years. Small baskets now sell for ten to twenty dollars, though most sewers keep on hand a number of five dollar items, such as bells, wreaths, Christmas stars, toy baskets, and the work of children. Middle-sized baskets range from thirty to eighty dollars, and very large baskets command prices in the hundreds and even thousands of dollars.

How many people the demand for baskets-as-art can support is uncertain, but the impact of this new market is likely to be great. Already we can see the drive to excel; the emphasis on regular stitching and elaborate surface decoration; the rise of innovation and the eclipse of the basket's historic provincialism and primitivism—results, albeit indirect, of pressures and tastes exerted by buyers looking for expressive forms.

To take advantage of new opportunities and deal collectively with their problems, the basketmakers formed the Mt. Pleasant Sweetgrass Basketmakers' Association in the spring of 1988. The association is a direct outgrowth of the Sweetgrass Steering Committee, an ad hoc group recruited to help organize the Sweetgrass Conference. Sponsored by the McKissick Museum at the University of South Carolina, with assistance from the Avery Research Center for Afro-American History and Culture and The Charleston Museum, the conference was funded by the National Endowment for the Arts and the Ruth Mott Foundation. This experiment in public-sector folklore sought to make people aware of the diminishing supply of sweetgrass and to develop strategies to assure the future of lowcountry basketmaking.

The conference convened on March 26, 1988, the morning after the field trip to Seabrook Island. Members of the Sweetgrass Steering Committee opened each panel and set a tone of deep commitment. They spoke about what basketmaking means to them and what it should mean to those outside the tradition. Sea grass basketry, explained Marguerite Middleton, "is an art form which demands and deserves the respect of the community and our state, for it is an integral part of our Afro-American heritage as well as our city's economy. . . . There is too much valuable history surrounding sweetgrass baskets to allow this art form to die."

A distinguished roster of folklorists, scientists, land managers, public officials, and community leaders shared information and proposed ways to expand the supply of sweetgrass and preserve the highway basket stands. The most pressing tasks, as defined at the conference, include a coastal survey of sweetgrass to identify existing sites and, wherever possible, to arrange for controlled harvesting; experimental propagation of the plant with a view toward large-scale cultivation; and the establishment of a "green corridor" along Highway 17 North to protect the basket stands.

"History must record this as a first," concluded Mrs. Middleton, "for never before have we had a meeting of this magnitude where weavers, lawmakers, and others in key decision-making positions have met to discuss issues which affect basketweaving." In his closing remarks, Congressman Ar-thur Ravenel, Jr., whose district includes Mt. Pleasant, succinctly stated a philosophy of development compatible with traditional arts. "Growth that preserves these valuable traditions," Ravenel proclaimed, "is fundamentally better than growth that does not." The audience breathed a hearty "Amen."

Where the initiatives outlined at the conference will lead remains to be seen. But the stakes are high. "Coiled basketry," expounded folklorist John Michael Vlach, "is a precious historical and cultural legacy, an expression of endurance and virtuosity. It shows us how people can give their best when they might be excused from making anything at all."

One thing we can count on is the basket-makers' sense of responsibility to the next generation, and to the generations that came before. "That responsibility," according to Mrs. Middleton, "has been none other than that of preserving the tradition of sweetgrass baskets. As history has proved, our people weaved in spite of the times. So it must be with our generation, for—it's *our* time now!"

Pocketbook, knitting basket, jewelry box, and sewing basket by Marilyn Dingle. Photograph by Theodore Rosengarten, June 1988

Basketweavers

BY JOYCE V. COAKLEY

At the Sweetgrass Conference held at The Charleston Museum in Charleston, South Carolina, on March 26, 1988, Joyce V. Coakley spoke movingly about the importance of basketmaking to her ancestors and to herself and her community today. The following excerpt is taken from that presentation.

Before the construction of the Cooper River Bridge [in the 1930s], the weavers fought against time and nature in order to take the goods to the market. For those living in the Seven-Mile/Hamlin Beach area, the typical day started at 3:30 A.M. Each adult family member was awakened to a set of predetermined chores. By 4:00 A.M. the ox-drawn wagon was ready for the two-and-a-half-hour journey down the rugged old Georgetown Highway. Sometimes they were met by wind, icy cold rain, mud holes in the road, snakes, and many other obstacles that tried to hamper them along the way. But there was not time for stopping because the Laurence and the Sappho ferry boats left the dock on time. These were the boats that were used to transport both people and livestock across the Charleston harbor.

But even with the hardship of transportation and the uncertainty of a sale, our grandparents kept forging on. At times they appeared so strong and oblivious to pain and suffering. Each day they went with the faith that God would supply their needs. As one grandmother recalls, there were days when the weather was so rough that it appeared that the ferry itself would be swept into the ocean, yet they had to keep fighting, for meals depended on the success of the market sales. This sacrifice of one's life was out of true love for the family. These were the precious days that we treasure so deeply in our hearts. When we consider the late nights that were spent trying to get a basket completed so that financial obligations could be met, we are grateful. There were many days when things looked grim. It seemed as though victory was in the hands of the enemy. Then one of the wise old grandparents, in an expression of faith, would remind the family that God was never a minute late or a penny short.

It appears that life should have been easier after the construction of the Cooper River Bridge and Highway 17, but these were hard days for everyone. At one time it appeared that the community would be decimated by poverty due to the national crisis. The hardship actually unified the community as each prayed for guidance and encouragement. The community would congregate in meeting halls called "The Classroom" for regular prayer services. It was at one of those meetings that Sam Coakley told the community that businessmen were looking for baskets to send to New York and other places in the North. Each family in the community was provided with the opportunity to trade. This made conditions a little more tolerable.

Meanwhile, other members of the community were still harvesting crops at the plantation in the community. It was a summer day when Ida Wilson got into a disagreement with one of the bosses and was invited off the property, that the first idea of selling baskets on Highway 17 was born. At the suggestion of her husband, she placed a few pieces on a chair and made a sale. She later shared this idea with her friends Edna Rouse, Betsy Johnson, and Jane Moultrie. These ladies got together with their husbands and designed the first basket stands. To this day the style remains the same. Despite the dismal state of affairs, the baskets have always offered the community a glimmer of hope.

With increasing determination, we strive to carry on this tradition. Not only are we proud of our weaving, but more importantly, we weave because we're proud.

*"Loading the Rice
Schooner." Watercolor by
Alice Ravenel Huger Smith.
Courtesy of the Carolina
Art Association/Gibbes
Museum of Art*

Contributors

Pamela Swing is a writer and public-sector folklorist who lives in Arlington, Massachusetts. She has visited the Shetland Islands of Scotland regularly since studying there on a college program, and is currently writing a Ph.D. dissertation on teaching traditional fiddle in Shetland Isles schools.

Ervin Beck is professor of English at Goshen College in Indiana. A specialist in English Renaissance literature, he has also written many articles on Belizean Creole songs and stories, English legends and customs, and Indiana Mennonite legends and Amish folk arts. His latest book is *Joe Wright: Goshen Folk Hero* (1988).

Erika Brady is adjunct professor of folklife and associate of the Center for Regional History and Cultural Heritage at Southeast Missouri State University. A Herbert E. Kahler Fellowship from Eastern National Park and Monument Association enabled Dr. Brady to pursue research on attitudes toward land use and wildlife in the Missouri Ozarks.

Mary Hufford is a folklife specialist at the American Folklife Center. She is the author of *One Space, Many Places: Folklife and Land Use in New Jersey's Pinelands National Reserve* (1986) and is currently writing a Ph.D. dissertation on fox hunting in the Pine Barrens.

Sally Peterson is a doctoral candidate in the University of Pennsylvania's Department of Folklore and Folklife and is writing a dissertation on traditional Hmong needlework. She has conducted fieldwork in Hmong communities in Pennsylvania, North Carolina, California, Washington, and Michigan.

Dale Rosengarten was guest curator for the McKissick Museum's Lowcountry Basket Project and is the author of the exhibition catalog, *Row Upon Row: Sea Grass Baskets of the South Carolina Lowcountry* (1986). During the winter of 1987–88, she served as director of the Sweetgrass Conference. *Row Upon Row* and the proceedings of the Sweetgrass Conference are available from McKissick Museum, The University of South Carolina, Columbia, S.C. 29208.

Jane Schwartz is a writer who lives in Brooklyn, New York. Her first novel, *Caught* (Available Press, 1985; Ballantine, 1987), used the world of the pigeon flyers as the background for the story of an unusual friendship between a ten-year-old girl and a grown man. Her second book is about the great thoroughbred filly Ruffian and will be published by Random House Inc. in 1990.

Marta Weigle is professor of American studies and anthropology at the University of New Mexico in Albuquerque. She is on the editorial boards of the Folklore and Society series of the University of Illinois Press, *Journal of Anthropological Research,* and *Journal of American Folklore* and is an editor for Ancient City Press in Sante Fe. Dr. Weigle is the author of many books and articles, including *Sante Fe and Taos: The Writer's Era, 1916–1941* (1982, with Kyle Fiore), *New Mexicans in Cameo and Camera: New Deal Documentation of Twentieth-Century Lives* (1985), and *The Lore of New Mexico* (1988, with Peter White).

David Whisnant is professor of English and American studies at the University of North Carolina, Chapel Hill. His books on the Appalachian region include *Modernizing the Mountaineer: People, Power and Planning in Appalachia* (1980) and *All That Is Native and Fine: The Politics of Culture in an American Region* (1983). He is currently at work on a book on cultural policy and the politics of culture in Nicaragua.

Don Yoder has been professor of folklore and folklife at the University of Pennsylvania since 1956. He is also adjunct professor of religious studies there. He was the editor of the journal *Pennsylvania Folklife* from 1961 until 1978 and the editor of the book *American Folklife* (1976). He is the author of many articles and books, including *Pennsylvania German Immigrants, 1709–1786* (1980) and, with Thomas E. Graves, *Hex Signs: Pennsylvania Dutch Barn Symbols and Their Meaning* (1989). Professor Yoder has been president of the American Folklore Society, a member of the first Board of Trustees for the American Folklife Center, and was recently elected to membership in the American Antiquarian Society.

Charles G. Zug III is professor of English at the University of North Carolina, Chapel Hill, where he also teaches in the Curriculum in Folklore. He has curated exhibitions of North Carolina pottery and folk art and written many articles for literary and folklore journals. Dr. Zug is the author of *Turners and Burners: The Folk Potters of North Carolina* (1986).

Publications of the American Folklife Center

Ethnic Heritage and Language Schools in America

1988. Developed by Elena Bradunas, compiled and edited by Brett Topping. 336 pp. Illustrated (S/N 030-001-00124-5) $16. Available from the Superintendent of Documents, U.S. Government Printing Office, Washington, D.C. 20402. Check or money order payable to the Superintendent of Documents must accompany order.

Thirteen articles that report on a project conducted by the American Folklife Center in 1982 to study a sampling of ethnic language schools at twenty different locations around the country. Such topics as history, school administration, parents, teachers, classes, curriculum, and the purposes of the school are discussed in each article.

The Federal Cylinder Project: A Guide to Field Cylinder Recordings in Federal Agencies

Available from the Superintendent of Documents, U.S. Government Printing Office, Washington, D.C. 20402. Check or money order payable to the Superintendent of Documents must accompany order.

VOLUME 1, 1984, INTRODUCTION AND INVENTORY, *by Erika Brady, Maria La Vigna, Dorothy Sara Lee, and Thomas Vennum, Jr. 110 pp. (S/N 030-000-00153-2) $8.50*

Introductory essay that describes the project and an indexed listing by collection of more than ten thousand field-recorded wax cylinders for which preservation tape copies exist at the Library of Congress.

VOLUME 2, 1985, NORTHEASTERN INDIAN CATALOG, *edited by Judith A. Gray;* SOUTHEASTERN INDIAN CATALOG, *edited by Dorothy Sara Lee, 432 pp. (S/N 030-000-00167-2) $14.*

Sixteen collections from northeastern Indian tribes, including the oldest collection of field recordings (the 1890 Passamaquoddy) and large collections of Chippewa, Menominee, and Winebago music recordings made by Frances Densmore; and six collections from southeastern Indian tribes, the largest of which is the Densmore Seminole collection.

VOLUME 3, 1988, GREAT BASIN/PLATEAU INDIAN CATALOG; NORTHWEST COAST/ARCTIC INDIAN CATALOG, *edited by Judith A. Gray, 304 pp. (S/N 030-000-00189-3) $17.*

Seven collections from the Great Basin and Plateau regions, the largest of which is the Frances Densmore Northern Ute material, and twenty collections from the Northwest Coast, Alaska, and Greenland, the largest of which is Densmore's Makah material. Leo Frachtcnbcrg's Quileute collection represents an early methodical effort to compare versions of individual songs as performed by different singers or by the same singer at different times.

VOLUME 8, 1984, EARLY ANTHOLOGIES, *edited by Dorothy Sara Lee, with a foreword by Sue Carole De Vale, 96 pp. (S/N 030-000-154-1) $8.*

Describes Benjamin Ives Gilman's cylinder recordings from the 1893 World's Columbian Exposition and the "Demonstration Collection" edited by Erich Moritz von Hornbostel and issued by the Berlin Phonogramm Archiv shortly after World War I.

Folklife Annual

Edited by Alan Jabbour and James Hardin. Available from the Superintendent of Documents, U.S. Government Printing Office, Washington, D.C. 20402. Check or money order payable to the Superintendent of Documents must accompany order.

1985. 176 pp. (S/N 030-000-00169-9) $16.

Articles on the New Jersey Pinelands, the Archive of Folk Culture at the Library of Congress, a lumber camp ballad, cowboy culture, Italian stone carvers, the Watts Towers in Los Angeles, and folk artist Howard Finster.

1986. 176 pp. (S/N 030-000-00179-6) $19.

Articles on breakdancing in New York City, filmmaking in Peru, whaling customs on a Caribbean island, the fiftieth anniversary of the *Kalevala* (the Finnish national epic), a logging camp in Minnesota, and the life story.

1987. 160 pp. (S/N 030-000-00202-4) $23.

Articles on the American Indian powwow, both in the United States and Canada; Afro-American folktales; private rituals of grief; and the Reverend C. L. Franklin; an interview with Texas folklorist John Henry Faulk; and reports on four ethnic heritage and language schools, Korean, German-Russian, Hupa Indian, and Islamic.

The Grouse Creek Cultural Survey

1988. By Thomas Carter and Carl Fleischhauer. 74 pp. Illustrated (S/N 030-000-00203-2) $5. For sale by the

Superintendent of Documents, U.S. Government Printing Office, Washington, D.C. 20402

The report of a survey of cultural resources conducted in Grouse Creek, Utah, July 1985, a joint project of the American Folklife Center, the Utah State Historic Preservation Office, the Folk Arts Program of the Utah Arts Council, the Western Folklife Center, the National Park Service, and Utah State University. The survey team included folklorists and architectural historians interested in finding a comprehensive approach to documenting and preserving America's cultural heritage.

Pennsylvania German Fraktur and Printed Broadsides: A Guide to the Collections in the Library of Congress

1988. Compiled by Paul Conner and Jill Roberts, with an introduction by Don Yoder. 48 pp. Illustrated. $9.95 plus $2.00 postage and handling. Available from the Library of Congress, Sales Shop, Washington, D.C. 20540. Check or money order payable to the Library of Congress must accompany order.

Lists 163 items of illuminated manuscripts and printed broadsides from the eighteenth and nineteenth centuries, located in the collections of the Library of Congress, principally in the Prints and Photographs Division.

Quilt Collections: A Directory for the United States and Canada

1987. By Lisa Turner Oshins. 255 pp. $24.95 hardcover; $18.98 softcover. Single copies available from the Library of Congress, American Folklife Center, Washington, D.C. 20540. Check payable to the American Folklife Center must accompany order. Add $2 per order for shipping and handling. Multiple copies available from Acropolis Books, Ltd., 2400 17th Street, N.W., Washington, D.C. 20009.

A guide to over 25,000 quilts and quilt study resources in 747 public collections. Illustrated in color and black and white.

The following publications are available free of charge from the Library of Congress, American Folklife Center, Washington, D.C. 20540.

American Folk Music and Folklore Recordings: A Selected List

Annual. 1984–87. An annotated list of recordings selected because they include excellent examples of traditional folk music.

American Folklife Center

A brochure on the services and activities of the Center.

Archive of Folk Culture

A brochure on the services and collections of the Archive.

El Centro Americano de Tradición Popular

The Center's general brochure in Spanish.

Ethnic Folklife Dissertations from the United States and Canada, 1960–1980: A Selected Annotated Bibliography

By Catherine Hiebert Kerst. 69 pp.

Brief abstracts of dissertations that examine the dynamic and complex processes by which ethnic groups maintain their identity in pluralistic societies, and information on obtaining access to these studies.

Folk Recordings: Selected from the Archive of Folk Culture

Brochure and order form.

Folklife Center News

A quarterly newsletter reporting on the activities and programs of the Center.

Folklife and Fieldwork: A Layman's Introduction to Field Techniques

By Peter Bartis, 28 pp.

An introduction to the methods and techniques of fieldwork.

An Inventory of the Bibliographies and Other Reference and Finding Aids Prepared by the Archive of Folk Culture

Information handout listing research materials at the Archive.

Tradición popular e investigación de campo

A Spanish translation of *Folklife and Fieldwork.*